The Problem
with
Adam & Eve

The Problem with Adam & Eve

by
Robert R. Davis

The Problem with Adam & Eve
© Copyright 2024, Robert R. Davis

All scripture quotations, unless otherwise indicated, are taken from the Holy Bible (King James Version). The author has inserted italics and bolding used in quotations from Scripture.

Table of Contents

Introduction

The story of Adam and Eve has shaped our view on morality and human nature almost worldwide. Even for people not strictly religious, the story of Adam and Eve provides a common reference point for understanding concepts like temptation, disobedience, and the consequences of choices.

Although, the Garden of Eden is a creation narrative designed to explain the origins of sin. "The story of Adam and Eve still has an uncanny influence on gender politics. The image of woman as evil temptress persists to this day, and not just in the religious sphere. Eve is an oft-employed motif in art, literature and music. However, in modern times, she is portrayed less as the negative feminine influence and more like a symbol of the bridge between innocence and experience, her story remains lodged in society's subconscious. Every time a woman is faulted for leading a man to evil thoughts or behavior, we are harking back to the era of Eden. The offensive notion that a woman can provoke rape or molestation by the way she looks is also a byproduct of this mentality. Strangely enough, this thought pattern exists in non-Biblical societies as well. The laws in many Muslim countries, which require women to cover up from head to toe, are based on a fear of women's seductress influence."[1]

There is a prevailing belief that every human problem has its roots in the Fall. The order in which Eve was created, and the fact that she was the first one to eat the forbidden fruit, has been held up as the reason why women must submit to men, even thousands of years later. Eve has been used as the reason for male domination since antiquity.

There are two different beliefs that churches hold when it comes to the role of men and women in ministry. Egalitarian-minded Christians believe that men and women are equals spiritually and that they can both minister, teach, and lead within the Church. Complementarian minded Christians believe that men and women are equal before God, but with different roles that complement each other. However, women cannot lead men in Church.

"The portrayal of Eve as an icon of feminine deceit is featured more in Christian liturgy than in Jewish works, which may be linked to Judaism's divergent interpretation of the Original Sin. According to the Torah, the story of Adam and Eve is far more complex than a simple "she led him to sin" tale. The sages explain that God commanded Adam not to eat from the Tree of Knowledge, and to relay the message to his wife. However, rather than entrusting Eve with God's exact commandment, Adam informed her that they were forbidden to *touch* the tree. He intended the addition as a safeguard, but the misinformation made Eve vulnerable to the trickery of the snake, who enticed her into sin by first proving that nothing bad will happen if she merely touches the tree. Thus, the birth of sin was not just the story of a seductive woman luring man into evil; it is also the world's first male-female miscommunication, laying the groundwork for many, many more to come. (This mistake was later rectified when, prior to the giving of the Torah, God commanded Moses to teach the laws to the women first.)

However, even if you reconcile the issue by placing equal blame, there is still the matter of the curses. Adam and Eve both received punishments for their transgression, affecting all men and women of future generations, but Eve's curses included the added shame of subordination. God said "And he shall dominate you." Nevertheless, even more troubling than the curse, is the way it has been used to justify maintaining the status quo of male dominance. Men and women contend that gender roles are woven into the fabric of creation, as if existence itself would somehow unravel if we were to end gender inequality."[2]

We cannot deny the fact that Eve was the first to succumb to temptation and she in turn tempted Adam. However, he was not an innocent bystander in all this. He knew the rules as well as her. However, just because we are in the 21st century does not change what the Bible teaches. Every prohibition of Paul against women leading or being a pastor is grounded in the story Adam and Eve. Therefore, we need to go beyond our Sunday School understanding of it and see what it really says.

In this book, we will take a deeper look at creation of humans. We will look at the roles of Adam and Eve in the garden. Lastly, we will see how actions of Eve have kept women from the pulpit.

The Name Adam

Genesis 1:26 *And God said, Let us make man in our image, after our likeness: and let them have dominion over the fish of the sea, and over the fowl of the air, and over the cattle, and over all the earth, and over every creeping thing that creepeth upon the earth.*
Genesis 1:27 *So God created man in his own image, in the image of God created he him; male and female created he them.*
Genesis 1:28 *And God blessed them, and God said unto them, Be fruitful, and multiply, and replenish the earth, and subdue it: and have dominion over the fish of the sea, and over the fowl of the air, and over every living thing that moveth upon the earth.*

The first thing we need to understand when we read the Bible in English is that we are viewing a translation. It is not verbatim what the original text says.

> Translation is the communication of the meaning of a source-language text by means of an equivalent target-language text. A translator always risks inadvertently introducing source-language words, grammar, or syntax into the target-language rendering.

In other words, a translation is an interpretation of the original text. That being the case, sometimes it misses the true meaning of the original writers.

The Bible was written in Hebrew (Old Testament), Aramaic (Old Testament) and Greek (New Testament). So, do we need to become fluent in these languages to

11

understand the Bible? Fortunately, we do not. Bible translations do most of the work for us. In order to find out the meaning of a few words here and there, we can use a concordance or a lexicon/dictionary.

In Genesis 1:26, we read, "And God said, Let us make man …" The word man in the concordance is transliterated as ādām.

Hebrew Strong's Number: 120

Hebrew Word: אָדָם
Transliteration: 'ādām
Phonetic Pronunciation: aw-dawm'
Root: from <H119>
Cross Reference: TWOT - 25a
Part of Speech: n m
Vine's Words: Man

Usage Notes:

English Words used in KJV:
    man 408
    men 121
    Adam 13
    person(s) 8
    common sort + <H7230> 1
    hypocrite 1
    [Total Count: 552]

from <H119> ('adam); *ruddy,* i.e. a *human being* (an individual or the species, *mankind,* etc.) :- × another, + hypocrite, + common sort, × low, man (mean, of low degree), person.

Figure 1. Strong's Concordance

It appears as H120 in the concordance. The "H" stands for Hebrew and 120 is the number assigned to the term. Looking at figure 1, we see the word is translated as "man" 408 times, "men" 121 times and "Adam" only 13 times. The differences come because of how the translators have interpreted the original text to English. Therefore, when we see the term Adam, this was the translator's decision to make it a proper name, not the original writers.

To complicate things even further, Strong's concordance also has another number H121, for the exact same Hebrew word.

Hebrew Strong's Number: 121

Hebrew Word: אָדָם
Transliteration: 'ādām
Phonetic Pronunciation: aw-dawm'
Root: the same as <H120>, Greek <G76>
Cross Reference: TWOT - 25a
Part of Speech: n pr m
Vine's Words: None

Usage Notes:

English Words used in KJV:
    Adam 9
    [Total Count: 9]

the same as <H120> ('adam); *Adam*, the name of the first man, also of a place in Palestine :- Adam.

Figure 2. Strong's Concordance

It seems as though they were attempting to separate the proper name usage of ādām from the generic sense of the word. However, they already have 13 instances of the proper name in H120. What is the difference? In the nine instances of H121, the writers seem to be referring to an individual or a city. It is not as clear-cut in the other H120 references.

Therefore, all in total there are 22 times when the translators switch from the generic term for man to the proper name of Adam. Now we are ready to look at our text again.

Genesis 1:26 And God said, Let us make man <H120> [ādām] in our image, after our likeness: and let them have dominion over the fish of the sea, and over the fowl of the

13

air, and over the cattle, and over all the earth, and over every creeping thing that creepeth upon the earth.

Genesis 1:27 So God created man <H120> [ādām] in his own image, in the image of God created he him; male and female created he them.

Genesis 1:28 And God blessed them, and God said unto them, Be fruitful, and multiply, and replenish the earth, and subdue it: and have dominion over the fish of the sea, and over the fowl of the air, and over every living thing that moveth upon the earth.

The first question we should ask is does the term man mean male? The answer is no. The term man is a generic and slightly archaic usage by today's standards. Looking at figure 1, we see the definition is human being, an individual or the species, mankind. In today's language, we would simply say humans.

In addition, in Genesis 1:27 the text states, God created man in His image ... male and female created He them. Therefore, if man only meant males why did He also create females? The text goes immediately from man (singular) to them (plural) in verses 26 through 28. This would be illogical if man only meant males.

However, look at how the text flows if we switch the translator's interpretation from man to humans.

Genesis 1:26 And God said, Let us make **humans** in our image, after our likeness: and let **them** have dominion over the fish of the sea, and over the fowl of the air, and over the cattle, and over all the earth, and over every creeping thing that creepeth upon the earth.

Genesis 1:27 So God created **humans** in his own image, in the image of God created he **them**; male and female created he **them**.

Genesis 1:28 And God blessed **them**, and God said unto **them**, Be fruitful, and multiply, and replenish the earth, and subdue it: and have dominion over the fish of the sea, and over the fowl of the air, *and over every living thing that moveth upon the earth.*

Now the text flows seamlessly from humans to them and from humans to male and female. However, this took a lot of research on our part for something seemingly so simple. Some might argue that this is an implicit example at best. Others may even disregard this example as being only my interpretation. We have seen that it makes logical sense, but I have heard people say not everything in the Bible makes sense.

I have asserted that āḏām represents both male and female in Genesis. In the first chapter of Genesis the writer is implicitly make this truth known. However, this truth is explicitly stated just a few chapters later.

Genesis 5:1 This is the book of the generations of Adam. In the day that God created man, in the likeness of God made he him;
Genesis 5:2 Male and female created he them; and blessed them, and called their name Adam, in the day when they were created.

Did you see in Genesis 5:2 it states, God called their name Adam? Is this the same translation we looked at in Genesis chapter one? Yes, it most certainly is the same. In fact, most people are unaware that these words are in the Bible.

The Bible explicitly states God called both male and female Adam, in the day they were created, referring to Genesis 1:26-28. Therefore, this is not simply my interpretation. This is what the Bible proclaims.

Why is this not taught in Churches? Whenever, Adam and Eve are mentioned, it is as if Genesis 5:2 does not exist. It is either spiritual blindness or selective memory.

We should look at this closer to see which concordance numbers are being used.

Genesis 5:1 This is the book of the generations of Adam <*H121*>[ādām]. In the day that God created man <*H120*>[ādām], in the likeness of God made he him;
Genesis 5:2 Male and female created he them; and blessed them, and called their name Adam <*H120*>[ādām], in the day when they were created.

Verse one, starts with the H121 usage because it refers to the generations of Adam. As I stated earlier the concordance created a separate number (H121) when the text seems to be referring to an individual or city.

The next two instances of the passage both use the number H120. The first instance renders it as man in English and the second makes it the proper name Adam. This is solely at the translator's discretion.

Again, look at how the text flows if we switch the translator's interpretation from man and Adam to humans.

Genesis 5:1 This is the book of the generations of **humans**. In the day that God created **humanity**, in the likeness of God made he them;

Genesis 5:2 Male and female created he them; and blessed them, and called their name **humans**, in the day when they were created.

Although verse one, starts with the generations of āḏām. It does not have to be translated into a proper name to make sense.

We should note Adam is never a proper name in the book of Genesis. The term āḏām is sometimes translated as man and other times Adam. This leads us to believe there is a distinction, but there is not. The translators of the Bible were attempting to clarify and make sense of the Hebrew text. In the first chapter of Genesis, the Hebrew "āḏām" was translated to man. In the garden story, chapters two and three, it becomes "Adam" a proper name, in contrast to the Woman. However, this is erroneous and leads us to wrong conclusions, as we will see later.

āḏām means male and female

The argument can be made that although the King James Version of the Bible is the most popular English translation. It is not the most accurate interpretation. So, let's look at how some other versions have translated the text.

The New Revised Standard Version (NRSV) of the Bible is a popular choice for academic and theological circles. It is a revision of the Revised Standard Version (RSV) that is considered accurate and inclusive, and it is based on contemporary biblical manuscripts.

New Revised Standard Version Updated Edition
Genesis 5:1 This is the list of the descendants of Adam.

When God created humans,[a] he made them[b] in the likeness of God.
Genesis 5:2 Male and female he created them, and he blessed them and called them humans[c] when they were created.

Footnotes
   a) 5.1 Heb *adam*
   b) 5.1 Heb *him*
   c) 5.2 Heb *adam*

The English Standard Version (ESV) is also a popular choice among biblical scholars and theologians who lean toward theological conservatism.

English Standard Version
Genesis 5:1 This is the book of the generations of Adam. When God created man, he made him in the likeness of God.
Genesis 5:2 Male and female he created them, and he blessed them and named them Man[a] when they were created.

Footnotes
   a) Genesis 5:2 Hebrew *adam*

I have included text from the Jewish Publication Society (JPS) version of the TANAKH (Jewish Bible) since they should be a reliable source in translating the Hebrew to English.

JPS Tanakh
Bereshit (Genesis) 5:1 This is the book of the generations of Adam. In the day that God created man, in the likeness of God made He him;

Bereshit (Genesis) 5:2 male and female He created them, and blessed them, and called their name Adam, in the day they were created.

This is not an exhaustive list by any means, but it serves to show this is not a private interpretation. When we see the proper name Adam or man in the book of Genesis, it should be updated to humans.

Adam in the book Genesis is not a proper name

Even without knowing the Hebrew behind our English translation, the Bible clearly tells us Adam represents both male and female. It tells us both implicitly and explicitly. If we look at both verses together, it is undeniable what is meant, when we see the term Adam.

Implicit Statement
Genesis 1:27 **So God created man [adam]** *in his own image, in the image of God created he him;* **male and female created he them.**

Explicit Statement
Genesis 5:2 **Male and female created he them;** *and blessed them,* **and called their name Adam,** *in the day when they were created.*

I will continue to repeat the truth of Adam being both male and female throughout this work, because it is a new concept to most.

19

The Garden Story

The traditional understanding of the Garden of Eden is a biblical description concerning the origin of sin. However, it is not a historic account, but rather a symbolic narrative concerning the creation of humans and origin of evil.

A proper biblical exegesis reveals that although the book of Genesis reads as history, it also implements a wide array of literary techniques that convey allegory, metaphor, and symbolism.

The story of Adam and Eve are integral to understanding our relationship with God and ultimately ourselves. In this narrative Adam still represents both male and female. However, we must remember when reading the story it is like looking at shorthand. It is full of symbolic language that must be unpacked in order to be fully understood.

In chapter one of Genesis we have God giving āḏām dominion over fish, fowl, cattle, every creeping thing and over the whole earth. Dominion is supreme authority or sovereignty. Sovereignty is controlling influence or freedom from external control. In other words, humans are the god of this world.

Psalms 82:6 I have said, Ye are gods; and all of you are children of the most High.

John 10:34 Jesus answered them, Is it not written in your law, I said, Ye are gods?

This declaration and dominion belongs to both male and female, according to Genesis 1:26-28. Both sexes are made in the image and likeness of God. So, let's delve into chapter two and see what it has to say.

Genesis 2:7 And the LORD God formed man of the dust of the ground, and breathed into his nostrils the breath of life; and man became a living soul.

Here the writer declares God shaped us from the ground. In other words, He molded us like a potter using clay and then breathed His life into us. This implies He gave us His Spirit.

Questions naturally arise from this description of creation. Is the writer telling us that the male was created first and then the female? Is the writer giving us a deeper look at creation and telling us there is a creation order? Let's look at the scripture a little closer.

Genesis 2:7 And the LORD God formed man <H120> [ādām] of the dust of the ground, and breathed into his nostrils the breath of life; and man <H120> [ādām] became a living soul.

The concordance indicates the term man is the same Hebrew word ādām that was used in chapter one. Therefore, this term represents both male and female. However, do we have this right?

We know that the woman will be created from man in just a few verses of this chapter. Why would the writer hide meanings within the story? Does this make any sense?

*Proverbs 25:2 **It is the glory of God to conceal a thing**: but the honour of kings is to search out a matter.*

There are many things hidden within the Word of God and it is our job, to pray for wisdom and understand them.

*1 Corinthians 2:6 Howbeit **we speak wisdom** among them that are perfect: **yet not the wisdom of this world**, nor of the princes of this world, that come to nought:*
*1 Corinthians 2:7 **But we speak the wisdom of God in a mystery, even the hidden wisdom**, which God ordained before the world unto our glory:*

We must gain spiritual understanding of texts whenever we read the Word of God. This is especially true of the Old Testament, because the full meaning could not be understood before the Messiah was revealed.

If we translated the text into today's language, it would read as follows.

Genesis 2:7 And the LORD God formed **humans** of the dust of the ground, and breathed into [their] nostrils the breath of life; and **humans** became living souls.

Ancient Eden and the Garden

After God creates humans He plants a garden eastward in Eden. The word Eden means pleasure or delight. In today's terms, this might be translated as garden of joy, happiness or gladness. This garden was planted east of what location?

To answer this question let's look at science. Most scientists agree that humans first evolved on the continent of Africa. The latest findings as of this writing, pinpoint Ethiopia. Since this country is on the eastern coast of the continent, we can simply say east of Africa.

23

The more important question is where does the Bible put Eden?

Genesis 2:10 *And a river went out of Eden to water the garden; and from thence it was parted, and became into four heads.*
Genesis 2:11 *The name of the first is Pison: that is it which compasseth the whole land of Havilah, where there is gold;*
Genesis 2:12 *And the gold of that land is good: there is bdellium and the onyx stone.*
Genesis 2:13 *And the **name of the second river is Gihon**: the same is it that compasseth the whole land of Ethiopia.*
Genesis 2:14 *And **the name of the third river is Hiddekel**: that is it which goeth toward the east of Assyria. And **the fourth river is Euphrates.***

We have a river that flows through Eden and breaks into four separate rivers, Pison, Gihon, Hiddekel (Tigris) and Euphrates. Luckily, two of the four rivers still exist. So, we have a reference point to help us.

The Pison river flows through Havilah this region is full of gold. One of the earliest and most significant gold-rich regions in the Middle East was ancient Egypt. The exact location of Havilah is debated, but some suggested locations are Western Arabia, Southwest of the Arabian Peninsula, Somalia or Northeast of Mesopotamia. However, scriptures do help us find a general location.

*Genesis 25:18 And they dwelt from **Havilah unto Shur, that is before Egypt, as thou goest toward Assyria**: and he died in the presence of all his brethren.*

The term before Egypt means facing Egypt. The only two countries that border Egypt are Libya and Sudan. Sudan has a larger gold reserve than Libya, but that alone is not enough to go on.

All we know about the Gihon River is that it compasses the whole land of Ethiopia. However, if we link it the land of Havilah, I believe it gives us some more clues. Sudan borders both Egypt and Ethiopia. If Sudan were Havilah, then it would serve to give us a north, south border for the west side of Eden. I believe the Nile River would serve as a modern day replacement for both the Pison and Gihon Rivers. Just for approximation purposes.

The Hiddekel River is better known as the Tigris River today. The river flows through modern day Turkey, Syria and Iraq. This river serves as a north, south border for the east side of Eden.

Last, the Euphrates River also flows through Turkey, Syria and Iraq. This river runs almost parallel to the Tigris.

If we use the Nile River as our western border and the Tigris and Euphrates rivers as our eastern border, then we only need to look at what is in between them. What countries are in that space? We have Somalia, Yemen, Saudi Arabia, Jordan, Syria, Israel, Lebanon and Turkey. Of all the countries, that I have listed Israel seems the most probable candidate to be the Garden of Eden. Eden in the Bible most likely encompassed a much larger area than the garden.

In addition, the region of Eden would predate the naming of the countries that exist today. It may even have existed prior to the movements that lead to continental drift.

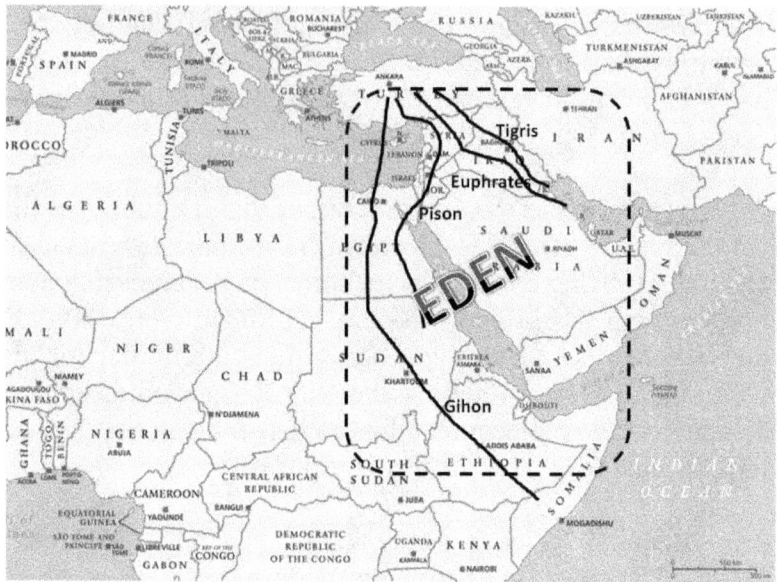

Figure 3. Eden Reimagined

It is important to note the Bible states, humans did not originate from Eden. For that reason, we took some time to find the probable location of Eden and its garden. Remember, at the current moment science believes Africa is the birthplace of humanity.

Genesis 2:15 *And the* LORD *God took the man, and put him into the garden of Eden to dress it and to keep it.*

We gloss over this scripture when we read, but I believe we miss a lot in doing so. Keep in mind, Adam is not a singular male figure. Adam represents both male and female.

Therefore, the question we need to ask is when God placed humans in the garden; did He use just one couple? This is unlikely. I think we imagine that God picked up Adam, like a G.I. Joe action figure and put him down in the garden, as children do with their toys. However, this is very unlikely.

When the Bible says, God took humans and put them in the garden. This is poetic language for the ancient human migration out of Africa.

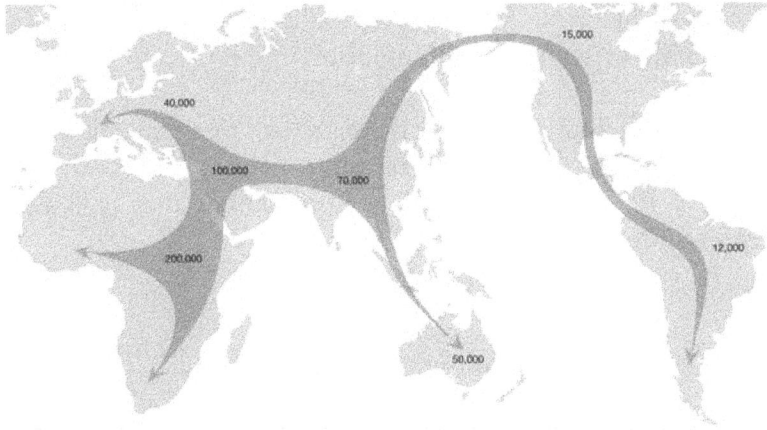

Figure 4. Ancient Human Migration. Credit: Peter Hermes Furian / Adobe Stock

It may be hard to see on the image, but it shows humans (Homo sapiens) originating around 200,000 years ago and the first migration occurring around 100,000 years ago. This means humans were around for over 100,000 years before the Eden story begins.

The only way we could get a single male figure in the Garden of Eden would be for God to transport him there miraculously. However, if humans migrated to Eden from Africa, it would be highly unlikely a solitary male made the trip. A successful migration would require a number of both males and females. Therefore, it is also doubtful that only one couple existed in Eden.

27

This goes against our literal understanding of the garden story. However, a symbolic narrative should never be interpreted literally.

The account of Adam and Eve is an allegory, which is a story that uses symbols to convey hidden meaning, typically a moral or political one. The word allegory comes from the Latin word allegoria, which means, "speaking to imply something else".

The literal interpretation of Adam and Eve is ubiquitous and incorrect. However, because everyone knows and accepts it, it has become a cultural belief that is almost impossible to change.

Dressing and Keeping the Garden

Genesis 2:15 And the LORD God took the man, and put him into the garden of Eden to dress it and to keep it.

In one simple sentence, the writer conveys to us the migration of humans out of Africa and a change of lifestyle and behavior.

Most take the fact that God put man in the garden to dress and keep it, as a divine mandate to work. Humans were to dress the garden. This comes from the Hebrew word *abhadh* meaning to work, till, cultivate, dress, and serve.

It is thought that we work because God worked. Since we were created in His image, this trait was passed down to us. Therefore, work is intrinsic to humans. This may be true, but is this what the story is trying to convey to us?

I do not believe this is the point of the text. The sentence goes from the migration of humanity, to working in the garden. It seems like something is missing. If we look at the word keep in Hebrew, it means to hedge about (as with thorns), i.e. guard; generally to protect, attend to something.

Humans are supposed to till and hedge (enclose) the garden. How does this relate to migration? The answer lies in why people migrated in the first place.

"Anthropologists have discovered evidence for the practice of hunter-gatherer culture by modern humans (*Homo sapiens*) and their distant ancestors dating as far back as two million years.

Because hunter-gatherers did not rely on agriculture, they used mobility as a survival strategy. Indeed, the hunter-gatherer lifestyle required access to large areas of land, between 7 and 500 square miles, to find the food they needed to survive. This made establishing long-term settlements impractical, and most hunter-gatherers were nomadic. These groups tended to range in size from an extended family to a larger band of no more than about 100 people."[3] In other words, migration is a direct byproduct of living a hunter-gatherer lifestyle.

The story states God put man in the garden to dress and keep it. This that means after humans migrated to Eden. They stopped foragering for food and transitioned to agriculture as a means to survive. Now we can see why Genesis 2:15 puts migrating and dressing/keeping the garden in one sentence. This is a lot of hidden meaning packed in one Bible verse.

The Commandment and the Two Trees

Genesis 2:9 *And out of the ground made the* LORD *God to grow every tree that is pleasant to the sight, and good for food; the tree of life also in the midst of the garden, and the tree of knowledge of good and evil.*

Genesis 2:16 *And the* LORD *God commanded the man, saying, Of every tree of the garden thou mayest freely eat:*
Genesis 2:17 *But of the tree of the knowledge of good and evil, thou shalt not eat of it: for in the day that thou eatest thereof thou shalt surely die.*

God commanded humans not to eat of the tree of knowledge of good and evil, but every other tree they were free to partake. This garden diet was actually a recapitulation of the original diet, with an added prohibition of the tree of good and evil.

In the beginning, humans were vegetarians according to Genesis chapter one.

Genesis 1:29 And God said, Behold, I have given you every herb bearing seed, which is upon the face of all the earth, and every tree, in the which is the fruit of a tree yielding seed; to you it shall be for meat.

"First things first, let's define our terms. A human is anyone who belongs to the genus *Homo* (Latin for man). Scientists still do not know exactly when or how the first humans evolved, but they have identified a few of the oldest ones.

One of the earliest known humans is *Homo habilis*, or "handy man," who lived about 2.4 million to 1.4 million years ago in Eastern and Southern Africa. Others include *Homo rudolfensis*, who lived in Eastern Africa about 1.9 million to 1.8 million years ago (its name comes from its discovery in East Rudolph, Kenya); and *Homo erectus*, the "upright man" who ranged from Southern Africa all the way to modern-day China and Indonesia from about 1.89 million to 110,000 years ago."[4]

Therefore, if the first humans were *Homo Habilis*, then they were vegetarians according to Genesis 1. The group God placed in the garden was most likely Homo sapiens. If this is true, then we can see why the command to be a vegetarian is reiterated in Genesis chapter two. "The first humans emerged in Africa around two million years ago, long before the modern humans known as *Homo sapiens* appeared on the same continent."[5]

Now we get to the origin of sin. Although the idea that Adam and Eve ate an apple is common today, the Book of Genesis never mentions the identity of the forbidden fruit. This led to a great deal of speculation among early Jewish and Christian commentators, and several species became popular candidates, primarily the fig and the grape and to a lesser extent the pomegranate and the citron (basically a lemon).

"Since at least the 17th-century, scholars have agreed that the answer is to be found in a quirk of the Latin language. The Latin word for apple is "malum," which happens to be a homonym of the Latin word for "evil." Since, the argument goes, the forbidden fruit caused the fall of man and humanity's expulsion from paradise, and it is certainly a terrible malum ("evil"). Therefore, what fruit is a more likely candidate than the malum, "apple"? This view has become conventional wisdom and is found in scholarly works across fields and disciplines."[6] However, there is no biblical support for this argument. In addition, the original text is Hebrew, not Latin. Therefore, the wordplay would not apply to the Hebrew text.

So, if the forbidden fruit is not an apple, what is it? Remember, whatever it is, it constitutes sin. Sin is a violation of God's will or an offense against His law. Up until this point in the book of Genesis, God has only given humans one commandment, to eat vegetarian.

Humans at some point began to eat meat. This changed us from purely gathers to hunter-gathers. Can the tree of knowledge of good and evil, refer to meat? Let's look a little closer at this theory.

"Fire control changed the course of human evolution, allowing our ancestors to stay warm, cook food, ward off predators and venture into harsh climates. It also had important social and behavioral implications, encouraging groups of people to gather and stay up late. When and where human ancestors learned how make fire remains a subject of debate and speculation. There is little consensus about which hominins—modern humans, a direct predecessor or a long-extinct branch—first acquired the skill."[7]

Science and history seems to corroborate meat eating had a significant impact on the size and thinking ability of the human brain. "Craig Stanford biological anthropologist and professor of Anthropology and Biological Sciences at USC make the assertion, our large brains gave us our exceptional thinking capacity and other distinctive characteristics, including advanced communication, tool use, and walking on two legs. Or was it the other way around? Did the challenges faced by early humans push the species toward communication, tool use, and walking and, in doing so drive the evolutionary engine toward a large brain? According to Stanford, what made humans unique was meat."[8] To be more specific, it was the cooking of meat, which provided the catalyst for human evolution, particularly the growth of the brain.

Early humans were eating raw meat from scavenging, long before they migrated to Eden. Is there any evidence that the people from the garden started cooking and eating meat?

"The oldest unequivocal evidence that humans could make fire, was found at Israel's Qesem Cave and dates back 300,000 to 400,000 years ago, associating the earliest control of fire with Homo sapiens and Neanderthals."[9] This finding puts us right back in our proposed location for the Garden of Eden, Israel.

All we have left to decode is the Tree of Life, which humans could freely eat. The tree of Knowledge of good and evil was not a literal tree and neither is the tree of life. So, what does it represent?

The Bible uses the term tree of life outside of the book of Genesis. Let's take a look at it.

Tree of Life

Wisdom	Proverbs 3:18
Fruit of Righteousness	Proverbs 11:30
Hope	Proverbs 13:12
Wholesome Tongue	Proverbs 15:4

The Hebrew term *etz chaim* (literally "tree of life") is a common one in Jewish life, often used to refer to the Torah. I think this is the best definition, but since the Torah did not exist in Eden, we will use the general term, Word of God.

In the book of Revelation, there are two trees in New Jerusalem, like the Garden of Eden, but this time there is no tree of knowledge of good and evil. It has been replaced with a second tree of life, a numeric allusion to Christ (2nd in the Godhead) being the true source of our eternal life. This time there is no chance to repeat the mistakes of Eden. Consequently, sin and death will never be a part of God's new creation.

Revelation 22:2 **In the midst of the street of it, and on either side of the river, was there the tree of life**, *which bare twelve manner of fruits, and yielded her fruit every month: and the leaves of the tree were for the healing of the nations.*

As we said earlier, the tree of life refers to the Word of God and two trees of life is a numeric allusion to Christ. Proof of this assumption is in the book of St. John.

John 1:14 And **the Word was made flesh**, *and dwelt among us, (and we beheld his glory, the glory as of the only begotten of the Father,) full of grace and truth.*

John states, Jesus is the Word made flesh. How does this relate to the tree of life analogy? In Genesis and Revelation, we can eat from the tree and receive eternal life. In the same manner, Christ is called the Bread of Life (St. John 6:35-51). We receive everlasting life by eating the bread, which is His flesh.

The Tree of Life and the Bread of Life are food metaphors, and eating represents obedience to the Word of God.

Adam still represents both male and female. Therefore, it is time to find out, who is the Woman?

34

<u>Who is the Woman?</u>

Genesis 2:18 And the LORD *God said, It is not good that the man should be alone; I will make him an help meet for him.*
Genesis 2:19 And out of the ground the LORD *God formed every beast of the field, and every fowl of the air; and brought them unto Adam to see what he would call them: and whatsoever Adam called every living creature, that was the name thereof.*
Genesis 2:20 And Adam gave names to all cattle, and to the fowl of the air, and to every beast of the field; but for Adam there was not found an help meet for him.

When we look at these verses, it is imperative that we remember males and females collectively are called Adam (humans). Keep in mind, many years have elapsed between Genesis chapter one and where we are now. Therefore, when humans name the animals they have been around for many thousands of years already.

Imagine Adam is a male, for a minute. Do we really believe God created man as an asexual being or did God realize late in the process this was not beneficial for man? This would mean woman was an afterthought of God. Are we implying the Lord is dull-witted? If the helper mentioned here is a female complement to Adam, what does that say about the all-knowing Creator? The literal explanation is problematic in reference to God.

The Lord created every other species with a male and female to complement each other, except Adam. Does this seem logical?

Furthermore, the scripture says Adam gave names to all of the creatures, which means he could talk. How did he develop a language in isolation? "In his famous course of lectures at the University of Geneva (1906-1911), de Saussure distinguished language as a system. It is a cultural institution, spoken and heard by individuals: language is not complete in any one speaker. It exists only within a collectivity...only by virtue of a sort of contract signed by members of a community."[10]

In other words, one individual alone cannot create a language. Therefore, it would be impossible for one person to name animals, if no one else existed. It would also be useless, because the next person to come along would not know any of the names.

I assert the creatures of the earth received their names from the male and female, called Adam. Together they named all creatures of the earth. We should take it a step further. I know this goes against conventional teaching, but if humankind has evolved to the point of speaking. We must remember language takes a long time to develop. Is it realistic for one couple to be alone on the earth?

Logically, there must be people scattered everywhere. If this were the case, other females would have to exist prior to Eve, in order to propagate the earth. God commanded man to be fruitful and multiply in Genesis chapter one. How could he obey the Lord without a female counterpart? It is just something to think about, as we continue to unfold the narrative.

God stated, "It is not good that the man should be alone; I will make him a help meet for him." We know that the term translated in this scripture as man is actually the Hebrew word "āḏām", which means male and female.

Therefore, it looks like God is saying it is not good for humans to be in isolation. In other words, we need community.

However, I believe it is much more than that. The Woman was created to be a help meet for Adam (male and female). First, we must understand there is no such thing as a "Helpmeet", which we render as "Helpmate" today. Helpmeet is not a word. The phrase is "help meet", which are two separate words. The word meet is an archaic English term, meaning suitable, right or proper. However, the footnote from the original King James Version has a notation indicating the meaning in Hebrew was "as before him". This means the term meet actually has the connotation of a face-to-face help.

Let's take a closer look at the term help. In Hebrew, the word is "Ezer". The meaning of this word is not simply help, but "succor". This one helps in times of hardship or distress. Ezer is used 21 times in the Old Testament. In almost every instance, God is the source of help.

When we see the Lord is our help, we understand the term to mean a very strong help. "Ezer" should not evoke images of docility, subservience or even equality. Quite the opposite it carries the connotation of military might, power or an unstoppable force that is greater than an individual. This knowledge alone should change our idea of who Eve is completely.

Genesis 2:21 And the LORD God caused a deep sleep to fall upon Adam, and he slept: and he took one of his ribs, and closed up the flesh instead thereof;
Genesis 2:22 And the rib, which the LORD God had taken from man, made he a woman, and brought her unto the man.

Genesis 2:23 And Adam said, This is now bone of my bones, and flesh of my flesh: she shall be called Woman, because she was taken out of Man.

Genesis 2:24 Therefore shall a man leave his father and his mother, and shall cleave unto his wife: and they shall be one flesh.

Genesis 2:25 And they were both naked, the man and his wife, and were not ashamed.

The language in this text is very figurative and as we have learned, we should not interpret it literally. Here we have the creation of the Woman.

Since the term, Adam embodies male and female, then who is the Woman? We have been taught she is Adam's wife and therefore "ādām" represents the male only, even though this clearly disagrees with scriptures (Genesis 1:27, 5:2), most still accept this teaching.

Genesis 2:23-24 cements the man wife ideology in our minds, because we use these verses in our marriage ceremonies. However, the apostle Paul declares this passage is a great mystery. When the Bible talks about something being a mystery, it is referring to a spiritual truth, which has been hidden somewhere in the scriptures.

Ephesians 5:32 This is a great mystery: but I speak concerning Christ and the church.

The apostle Paul talks about mysteries throughout his writings, but he rarely ever calls something a great mystery. This highlights its importance. He states, the husband, wife allegory refers to Christ and the Church. Most people accept this as truth. However, is the mystery about a husband and wife in general or does it refer to Adam and Eve?

38

*1 Corinthians 15:45 And **so it is written, The first man Adam was made a living soul; the last Adam was made a quickening spirit.***
1 Corinthians 15:46 Howbeit that was not first which is spiritual, but that which is natural; and afterward that which is spiritual.
*1 Corinthians 15:47 **The first man is of the earth, earthy: the second man is the Lord from heaven.***
1 Corinthians 15:48 As is the earthy, such are they also that are earthy: and as is the heavenly, such are they also that are heavenly.
1 Corinthians 15:49 And as we have borne the image of the earthy, we shall also bear the image of the heavenly.

The mystery seems to go deeper than simply husbands and wives. There is a first Adam, who is from the book of Genesis and there is a second or last Adam, who is Jesus. The first is from the earth and the last is from heaven. The parallel is deliberate, but why? The last Adam restores everything the first one lost. This is the mission of Christ.

For this reason, I believe the great mystery Paul describes is about Adam and Eve, not merely husbands and wives. Since, the two Adams are paralleled it makes it easier for us to decipher. If we look closely at how they parallel we should be able clear up the great mystery.

1. God causes Adam to sleep and opens his side
2. The Woman is formed from Adam
3. God presents the Woman to Adam as his bride

God causes Adam to sleep and opens his side

First, God causes Adam to fall into a deep sleep and then He opens up his side. What is the significance of this action? In the Bible, the term deep sleep can refer to death. By opening the side of Adam, God is symbolically taking the breath or life from him to create the Woman.

Most translations state God took one of Adam's ribs and made a woman. "However, according to Ziony Zevit, Distinguished Professor of Biblical Literature and Northwest Semitic Languages at American Jewish University in Bel-Air, California, "rib" is the wrong translation for *tsela* in the story of Adam and Eve. He believes that it should be translated as "a non-specific, general term," in other words, simply side."[11]

Hebrew Strong's Number: 6763

Hebrew Word: צֵלָע
Transliteration: sēlā'
Phonetic Pronunciation: tsay-law'

Hebrew Word: צְלָעָה
Transliteration: tsal'āh
Phonetic Pronunciation: tsal-aw'

Root: from <H6760>
Cross Reference: TWOT - 1924a
Part of Speech: n f
Vine's Words: None

Usage Notes:

English Words used in KJV:
        side 19
        chamber 11
        boards 2
        corners 2
        rib 2
        another 1
        beams 1
        halting 1
        leaves 1
        planks 1
        [Total Count: 41]

or (feminine) *tsal'ah*, tsal-aw'; from <H6760> (tsala'); a *rib* (as *curved*), literal (of the body), or figurative (of a door, i.e. *leaf*); hence a *side*, literal (of a person) or figurative (of an object or the sky, i.e. *quarter*); architecturally a (especially floor or ceiling) *timber* or *plank* (single or collective, i.e. a *flooring*) :- beam, board, chamber, corner, leaf, plank, rib, side (chamber).

Figure 5. Strong's Concordance

Strong's concordance only translates the Hebrew term *tsela* as rib twice in the Old Testament and both are in Genesis chapter two. Most of the time the term is translated as side.

In parallel to Adam, God caused Jesus to fall into a deep sleep, which indicates His death on the cross. This was also the work of God. John states, "For God so loved the world that he gave his only begotten Son." After, Jesus the last Adam is in a deep sleep, His side is also opened.

*St. John 19:33 But when **they came to Jesus, and saw that he was dead already**, they brake not his legs:*
*St. John 19:34 But **one of the soldiers with a spear pierced his side**, and forthwith came there out blood and water.*

By pouring out the blood and water from Jesus, God is symbolically taking the life from Him to create the Church. The first Adam relates to the physical creation of the Woman. The last Adam correlates to her spiritual formation.

The Woman is formed from Adam

God creates the Woman from Adam. Remember, the Bible declares, āḏām is a term denoting both male and female. God created the Woman, but she cannot be a literal female, since the gender already exists.

Think about this, would God command Adam to be fruitful and multiply (Genesis 1:28), without giving him the means to reproduce? That would be putting the cart before the horse, so to speak. Do we think God has dementia, of course not?

41

It is important to note, the Hebrew word "Asah" translated "made" is used in the creation story for every living thing God created, except the formation of the Woman. This seems odd, but let's not jump to conclusions.

The Hebrew word "Banah" is used for the Woman, which means to build. This is the first time we see the word used in the Bible, the next place is Genesis 4:17 when Cain builds a city. Curiously, the Woman is built, but the rest of creation is made.

Hebrew Strong's Number: 1129

Hebrew Word: בָּנָה
Transliteration: bānâ
Phonetic Pronunciation: baw-naw'
Root: a primitive root
Cross Reference: TWOT - 255
Part of Speech: v
Vine's Words: Build (To)

Usage Notes:

English Words used in KJV:
    build 340
    build up 14
    builder 10
    made 3
    built again + <H7725> 2
    repair 2
    set up 2
    have children 1
    obtain children 1
    surely (inf. for emphasis) 1
    [Total Count: 376]

a primitive root; to *build* (literal and figurative) :- (begin to) build (-er), obtain children, make, repair, set (up), × surely.

Figure 6. Strong's Concordance

The term *banah* is translated to "made" only 3 times. Once for the woman (Eve) and the other two times still pertain to building.

*Genesis 2:22 And the rib, which the LORD God had taken from man, **made** <H1129> he a woman, and brought her unto the man.*

*Ezekiel 27:5 They have **made** <H1129> all thy ship boards of fir trees of Senir: they have taken cedars from Lebanon to make masts for thee.*

*1 Kings 22:39 Now the rest of the acts of Ahab, and all that he did, and the ivory house which he **made** <H1129>, and all the cities that he built, are they not written in the book of the chronicles of the kings of Israel?*

This means the translators were well aware of the meaning of the Hebrew word, but they simply needed to make sense of the story. By changing the word from build to made, they inadvertently deepened the mystery that Paul alluded to in Ephesians.

To build means to form by ordering and uniting materials by gradual means into a composite whole. This means it took some time to form the Woman. It was not an instantaneous manifestation, which is why Adam needed to be in a deep sleep.

What did God build from Adam? The Woman here also represents a city. Since she is built from Adam prior to the original sin, the city is therefore holy. This is the original Holy City of God, long before Jerusalem. Can we prove this assumption?

Yes, what is true of the first Adam must also be true of the last one. Otherwise, we have broken the parallel. This assumption if proved will turn our understanding of the garden event upside down. If the Woman is a city, then there were many people in the garden, when the serpent spoke.

After Jesus died on the cross, a soldier opened His side with a spear. This act is symbolic of the formation of the Church. This entity was also built, not made.

*St. Matthew 16:18 And I say also unto thee, That thou art Peter, and upon this rock **I will build my Church**; and the gates of hell shall not prevail against it.*

The building of the Church is also a gradual work. The Church was not presented to Jesus immediately after His resurrection. In fact, it is still a future event. Note: The Woman in both cases took thousands of years to build.

Concerning the Church the apostle Paul states, Jerusalem above is our mother (Galatians 4:22-26). This means, New Jerusalem is the city and the Church members represent the inhabitants. However, the two terms are interchangeable. Therefore, building the Church and building the city New Jerusalem are indistinguishable.

Jesus told His disciples that He was going away to prepare or build a place for them (St. John 14:2-3). The Woman He is building is New Jerusalem. There is a definite duality in Jesus' roles. As the last Adam, He is still in a deep sleep, but as our Lord He is building His bride.

As I stated earlier, what is true of the first Adam must be true of the last. Therefore, since the Woman represents the Holy City with Jesus, the same must be true of the first Adam. This is indeed a Great Mystery, as Paul has declared.

God presents the Woman to Adam as his bride

In the last point, after Adam is awakened God presents the Woman to him as his bride. Adam declares the Woman is bone of his bone and flesh of his flesh, meaning the two are one.

Subsequently, Adam renames the Woman and calls her Eve, because she is the mother of all living. Paul declares the same concerning the Church. He states, Jerusalem above is the mother of all of us.

<u>Jerusalem called the mother of all</u>
*Galatians 4:26 But **Jerusalem which is above** is free, which **is the mother of us all**.*

<u>Jerusalem renamed by Christ</u>
*Revelation 3:12 Him that overcometh will I make a pillar in the temple of my God, and he shall go no more out: and I will write upon him the name of my God, and **the name of the city of my God, which is new Jerusalem**, which cometh down out of heaven from my God: and I will write upon him my new name.*

Most of us do not realize the term "new Jerusalem" comes directly from Jesus. In fact, the term is only found in the Bible twice and both are in the book of Revelation.

	First Adam	**Last Adam**
Taken from Adam's side	Bone and Flesh	Blood & Water
Woman formed from Adam	Physical	Spiritual
God presents the Woman to Adam	First Holy City	Last Holy City
Adam renames the Woman	Eve	New Jerusalem

The writer stated, "It is not good that the man should be alone; I will make him a help meet for him." It looks like God is saying it is not good for humans to be in isolation. In other words, we need a structured social community or simply society.

"Humans need society because it is essential for our survival and well-being, allowing us to cooperate, share resources, protect each other from threats, and develop our individual potential through social interaction; essentially, our evolutionary history has ingrained a need for social connection to thrive in a complex world."[12]

"Our need for social connection is rooted deep within us biologically not just as individuals, but also as a species. In fact, as an astonishing amount of theory and research now suggests, humans have evolved the need for social connection."[13]

Therefore, the help meet that God created for Adam was the Holy City (Woman). The city that was built from Adam was meant to be a mighty power and advocate for humanity. It was the original Kingdom of God.

This is why Jesus spoke of us saying, "We will do His works and even greater works." The greater works is what the body of Christ carries out. Jesus could only do so much physically because of the limitations of time and space, but the Kingdom of God is virtually unlimited.

Christ carries the thought of an "Ezer" forward with the Holy Spirit. He said He would leave us the "Comforter", which is better translated Helper. Just as God in the Old Testament was our help in the times of hardship or distress, The Holy Ghost is our ever-present Help today.

46

As I stated earlier, the whole purpose of Jesus' ministry is restoration. How can Christ the last Adam restore the Holy City to us, if the first Adam never had one? Think about it. If New Jerusalem is only replacing the current one, what part do we (Gentiles) have in it? Jerusalem is the Holy City of Israel, not the Church. I know God includes us by faith via Christ. However, Jerusalem holds little relevance to non-Jews. By that, I mean it is not our homeland.

In addition, we did not lose Jerusalem through Adam's sin. Jesus Christ came to restore what was lost, due to the fall of Adam. Every other covenant and work of God is towards this end. Therefore, the Woman in the garden was the original Holy City of God.

When we look at Eve, we are looking at the making of a human settlement of a substantial size, not a physical woman. Therefore, when God says, it is not good that humans are alone. He created a city to be their help meet.

A city is a type of local government entity. The primary purpose of a government is to be an institutional authority that rules a community of people. It maintains the welfare and security of its citizens and provides a framework for the orderly functioning of society. Remember, our earlier definition of "Ezer" (help meet). It carries the connotation of military might, power or an unstoppable force that is greater than the individual. Clearly, the Woman (Kingdom of God) the Lord created is the help meet humans needed.

Eve is the city of God and not an actual female. This great mystery has been hidden for centuries. Eve was built from both male and female. Otherwise, how would God populate the city? This is why the Woman is bone of my bone and flesh of my flesh. They are offspring.

47

Therefore, Adam represents both male and female in the creation of the Woman. The sexes are equal in this symbolic narrative and it has been that way from the beginning. Now we can clearly see the Hebrew term "Banah" (build) was not a mistake in connection to the Woman.

Let's see what all of this means in connection to the fall of humanity. Now that we know for sure, there were more than two people at the time of the original sin.

The Fall

Genesis 3:6 *And when the woman saw that the tree was good for food, and that it was pleasant to the eyes, and a tree to be desired to make one wise, she took of the fruit thereof, and did eat, and gave also unto her husband with her; and he did eat.*

Genesis 3:7 *And the eyes of them both were opened, and they knew that they were naked; and they sewed fig leaves together, and made themselves aprons.*

We know the Woman is a city and not a literal female, so how can she be tempted or commit sin. Eve is the first holy city of God. Is it biblically correct to say an entity, such as a city can commit a sin?

To answer this question we only have to look at Israel. Can Jerusalem ever be guilty of sinning?

Lamentations 1:8 ***Jerusalem hath grievously sinned;*** *therefore she is removed: all that honoured her despise her, because they have seen her nakedness: yea, she sigheth, and turneth backward.*

Although we are looking at a symbolic narrative, it is biblically correct to portray a city sinning. Therefore, it is acceptable to have the Woman commit a sin, even though we know she is not an actual female.

So, let's move on to why the Woman sinned. The tree of knowledge of good and evil was desirable to make one wise. Why would the city or its leaders desire to be wise? What is really behind this symbolism? The answer is in the punishment of the Woman. Her desire will be to her

49

husband and he will rule over you (Genesis 3:16). Are we just grabbing this conclusion out of the air? Does the Bible substantiate it?

Deuteronomy 1:13 ***Take you wise men****, and understanding, and known among your tribes,* ***and I will make them rulers over you.***

This seems like a legitimate desire to have wisdom in order to rule over God's people. It is hard to see why this would be a sin.

As we said, a city of a type of government, but what type would be appropriate for God's people. God's choice of government for His people is always a theocracy.

> **Theocracy** - government by divine guidance or by officials who are regarded as divinely guided. In many theocracies, government leaders are members of the clergy, and the state's legal system is based on religious law. Theocratic rule was typical of early civilizations.

When Israel entered the Promised Land, they were governed as a theocracy. The Lord placed judges over His people and God was the ruler.

In the Bible, a "judge" is a temporary, regional leader who primarily arose to deliver the Israelites from oppression during times of crisis, often with military leadership. Judges had limited, regional authority, often only active when a specific threat arose, while kings had power over the entire nation. Judges served for a specific period, only as long as the crisis lasted, whereas kings ruled for a lifetime and passed on their position to their heirs. God, not people, chose judges. In addition, a judge could not choose their successor.

How was a judge different from a prophet? Prophets in the Bible received messages from God to give to the people. This gave them religious authority, but not civil or military authority. Compared to prophets, the judges had a much more active role in the military affairs of Israel.

Therefore, God governed His people through judges and prophets that He assigned. The choice was not based off human wisdom, but the Lord searches the heart of men. This is where the Woman (city of God) went wrong. She wanted wisdom to rule the people, usurping the sovereignty of God. This act is most certainly sin.

God granted dominion to humans over everything He created, with the exception of humanity. As the children of the Almighty, we are His highest creation and the gods of this planet. This is indeed a noble calling. Just because the world is ours, does not mean we should treat it anyway we want. God has entrusted the earth to us. This implies that we are to be responsible with it. The world is God's gift to us. This is what makes the Gospel good news.

We are supposed to replenish the earth's resources, not deplete them. However, it goes further than that, as the gods of this world, we are supposed to restore everything the planet is lacking. For instance, when the world seems cold and indifferent, we renew it with love. When violence is on the upswing, we re-establish peace and so on. Being the god of this world implies responsibility.

The last piece of our purpose is to subdue the earth. This is a military term. It means to conquer, vanquish, defeat or overcome. "Every bird, fish and creature is to be in subjection to the authority of mankind. A conquering nature resides inside man, in order for them to subdue the earth. This is the reason that humans seeks to climb the highest mountain, explore outer reaches of space and push themselves to the limit."[14] We are also supposed to conquer or overcome our sinful nature, also known as the flesh. If you read the Letters to the seven churches in the book of Revelation, you will notice the phrase, "to him that overcomes," stated repeatedly. The most important thing to subdue in this life is our flesh (self).

This conquering nature was supposed to be balanced with the Spirit of God. However, when humans fell (sinned) God removed His Spirit and they died (spiritually). The balance was lost and the conquering nature of humanity became disproportionate. Now humans seek to dominant other humans. This was never in God's will. Whenever we attempt this, we are making ourselves equal with God. This was Eve's true motivation for eating the forbidden fruit. We were created to be like God, not His equal.

When humans lost their righteous standing before God, they gained an unwanted sinful nature through their disobedience. Consequently, we have never realized the true potential God has given to us to rule (peacefully). Due to sin, humanity lost their righteous stance before the Lord. However, God through His Son will restore righteous dominion to the earth.[15]

Other Effects of Sin

When humans ate from the tree of knowledge of good and evil, they in essence opened up a type of Pandora's Box. Fire gave humans the ability to eat meat on a regular basis. Ancient people became hunters, and not merely forgers.

Since all of this stemmed from eating meat, does God want us to be vegetarians? No, if we believe this, then we are missing the real point. If God's eternal purpose is for us to be meat free, Jesus would have been a vegetarian from birth. Jesus said, "The Son of man came eating meat and drinking; and you say, Behold a gluttonous man, and a winebibber, a friend of publicans and sinners!"[16] Furthermore, Christ gets right to the point in the book of Mark.

*St. Mark 7:18 And he saith unto them, **Are ye so without understanding** also? Do ye not perceive, **that whatsoever thing from without** entereth into the man, it **cannot defile him;***
*St. Mark 7:19 **Because it entereth** not into his heart, but **into the belly, and goeth out into the draught [toilet], purging all meats?***

If eating meat cannot defile us, why did God make all the fuss about eating meat in garden? God expelled Adam and Eve from paradise over meat. However, now we can eat everything under the sun without spiritual repercussions. Am I missing something?

They broke a command of God. Why did the Lord command them not to eat meat? What they did not take into account was the unspoken law of reciprocity.

Every living thing on the planet adheres to the covenant of sowing and reaping, without exception. This is one fundamental ordinance that governs the world. Reciprocity is the law, for all life on this planet and it is always in force. God put this law in place to benefit humanity. One seed produces countless pieces of fruit. This law enables humans to operate like Him, by faith. By simply planting

53

our word through faith, we would almost effortlessly reap a bountiful harvest.

The fall of man caused us to experience the bad side of reciprocity. Prior to the fall, humans were sinless and could sow only good seeds. Once we became familiar with evil, we immediately began to reap its harvest. This set the course of humanity on fire.

Once humans started killing animals in order to eat, we inadvertently sowed the seeds of violence and murder. After the fall, the next tragedy we see is the murder of Abel by his brother Cain and it has been this like this, ever since. This is why God commanded humans to eat as an herbivore. Adam as the god of the earth violated their purpose by killing. By doing so, humankind reaped a harvest they never envisioned.

The Loss of Innocence

"When Adam and Eve sinned the Bible says their eyes were opened. The next statement says they realized they were naked and then further, they decided to make clothes.

Their sin affected the way Adam and Eve perceived things. In fact, the shame they now felt was due to their new sinful nature, because they no longer perceived things in a perfect fashion. Hence, they viewed that their nakedness needed to be covered.

Note, nakedness was not a sin, but a fallen perception of nakedness and the associated shame was included in the sorrows and mental anguish they now felt. Even today, nakedness is bonded with shame, as people the world over wear clothes. In other words, their innocence was lost and once gone it cannot be regained."[17]

When humans ate of the tree knowledge of good and evil, they gained a familiarity by experience and it could never be undone. Knowledge of the good was not a problem. However, knowledge of evil or sin is a huge issue. Evil brings sorrow, distress and calamity with it. According to the Bible, this knowledge became our new nature through Adam. It is commonly called the Adamic or sin nature.

It is important to note in Genesis 3:22, God said, man is become as one of us, to know good and evil. Therefore, He put them out of the garden before they could gain immortality by eating the tree of life. Remember, humans were created in the image and likeness of God. It seems like humans may have been allowed to eat from the tree of knowledge of good and evil eventually. Perhaps we needed a higher level of maturity before we could handle it or as science calls it, evolution. This is not something we are going to know in this lifetime.

We have established whom Adam and Eve represent. However, some may believe the narrative switches between allegory and literalism. So, let's look at the different levels of possible meanings and decide which one makes the best sense. The levels we will view are literal, symbolic and spiritual. There may not always be three levels, but there will always be at least two.

The Penalties of Sin for the Woman

Genesis 3:16 Unto the woman he said, I will greatly multiply thy sorrow and thy conception; in sorrow thou shalt bring forth children; and thy desire shall be to thy husband, and he shall rule over thee.

The Woman received a threefold penalty for partaking of the forbidden fruit.

1. In sorrow you will bring forth children
2. Your desire will be to your husband
3. Your husband will rule over you

1. In sorrow you will bring forth children

Literal Meaning:
The literal interpretation believes there was an actual tree that Eve ate from, possibly an apple tree.

Does this make sense? Why would eating fruit cause conception issues in women? I cannot think of a valid reason for this to happen. There should be a cause and effect relationship.

Symbolic Meaning:
Earlier I postulated that eating from the forbidden fruit was actually symbolic of eating meat. We saw that meat eating had a significant impact on the size and thinking ability of the human brain. A bigger brain requires a larger head. Consequently, women have difficultly during conception.

Does this make sense? The logic holds up as to why the woman would have difficulty in birth.

Spiritual Meaning:
Remember, when we look at the Woman, we are referring to the city of God. Therefore, we must look at the next birth of God's people. According to the Bible, this would

be the birth of Israel. This process was long and arduous. The Israelites were born out of Egypt after 400 years of slavery.

Does this make sense? Scriptures confirm the birth of Israel resulted in suffering for the people of God.

2. Your desire will be to your husband

Literal Meaning:
This clause is confusing to say the least. I would think that a woman desiring her husband would be natural, not a curse.

"The Hebrew phrase in question does not include a verb and is literally translated "toward your husband your desire." Since this judgment is predictive, the future tense verb "will be" is added for clarity: "Your desire will be for your husband." The most basic and straightforward understanding of this verse is that woman and man would now have ongoing conflict. In contrast to the ideal conditions in the Garden of Eden and the harmony between Adam and Eve, their relationship, from that point on, would include a power struggle. The NLT translation makes it more evident: You will desire to control your husband, but he will rule over you.

God's pronouncement of this curse on the first couple signals a change in the marriage dynamic. Sin had wrought discord. The battle of the sexes had begun. Both man and woman would now seek the upper hand in marriage. The man who was to lovingly care for and nurture his wife would now seek to rule her, and the wife would desire to wrest control from her husband."[18]

This type of explanation comes from us trying to make sense of the literal interpretation of Adam and Eve. The Tanakh (Jewish Bible) keeps it simple. "Yet your urge shall be for your husband, and he shall rule over you."

Does this make sense? There is no curse involved, if we take the literal view that Eve represents an actual female. A wife should desire her husband.

Symbolic Meaning:
The Woman represents God's people and the husband is humanity. This means God's people will desire human leadership over God and this is both a prophecy and a curse, fulfilled by Israel. Therefore, this pronouncement was predictive.

*1 Samuel 10:19 And **ye have this day rejected your God**, who himself saved you out of all your adversities and your tribulations; and **ye have said unto him, Nay, but set a king over us.** Now therefore present yourselves before the LORD by your tribes, and by your thousands.*

Does this make sense? Scriptures confirm that Israel desired human leadership over God.

Spiritual Meaning:
The symbolic and spiritual meanings are the same. As I said, God's people will desire human leadership over His direction.

*Mark 7:8 **For laying aside the commandment of God, ye hold the tradition of men**, as the washing of pots and cups: and many other such like things ye do.*
*Mark 7:9 And he said unto them, **Full well ye reject the commandment of God, that ye may keep your own tradition.***

Does this make sense? Jesus spoke these words against Israel, but they still ring true for the Church today.

3. Your husband will rule over you

Literal Meaning:
I believe Benson's Commentary, which is a five-volume commentary on the Bible, hits the nail on the head, as far as how the literal meaning has been applied throughout history. This seems to be the clarion call for men to be in charge.

"Thy desire shall be to thy husband – That is, as appears from Genesis 4:7, where the same phrase is used, Thy desires shall be referred or submitted to thy husband's will and pleasure, to grant or deny them as he sees fit. **She had eaten of the forbidden fruit**, and thereby had committed a great sin, in compliance with her own desire, **without asking her husband's advice or consent,** as in all reason she ought to have done in so weighty and doubtful a matter, and therefore she is thus punished. He shall rule over thee — Seeing for want of thy husband's rule and guidance thou wast seduced, **and didst abuse the power and influence** I gave thee, **by drawing thy husband into sin**, thou shalt now be brought to a lower degree; and **whereas thou wast made thy husband's equal, thou shalt henceforward be his inferior, and he shall rule over thee — As thy lord and governor.**"[19]

Many societies and religions throughout history and even today seem to be operating as if this is a decree from God.

Does this make sense? This punishment seems logical, but the biblical reasoning for it does not.

*1 Timothy 2:14 And **Adam was not deceived, but the woman being deceived was in the transgression**.*
1 Timothy 2:15 Notwithstanding she shall be saved in childbearing, if they continue in faith and charity and holiness with sobriety.

If Adam was not fooled, but Eve was tricked or misled, doesn't this mean he has committed the greater sin? Even, if the apostle means she was beguiled and Adam was not, it still implies there is deception involved. If Adam was not fooled, this means he willfully did it. He made a conscious decision to disobey God and follow the Woman. Adam who committed the greater sin, now rules over the Woman. This does not make sense to me, nor does it seem fair.

Symbolic Meaning:
Again, the Woman represents God's people and the husband is humanity. This means God's people will be ruled by humans and not by God. This is indeed a curse and not the divine will of the Lord.

Does this make sense? Remember, God's choice of government for His people was always a theocracy. If you think this applies only to the Old Testament, observe what Jesus has to say about it.

*Mark 10:42 But Jesus called them to him, and saith unto them, Ye **know that they which are accounted to rule over the Gentiles exercise lordship over them**; and their great ones exercise authority upon them.*
*Mark 10:43 **But so shall it not be among you**: but whosoever will be great among you, shall be your minister:*
Mark 10:44 And whosoever of you will be the chiefest, shall be servant of all.

Mark 10:45 For even the Son of man came not to be ministered unto, but to minister, and to give his life a ransom for many.

In these verses, Jesus is not only talking about the desire to be great, but He is referring to His coming Kingdom or the government of God (see also St. Matthew 20:21-28, St. Luke 22:24-30). Christ is drawing a sharp contrast between human government and the kingdom of God. Humans were never meant to lord over or have absolute control over each other. This is true especially of God's people, both then and now.

Spiritual Meaning:
The symbolic and spiritual meanings are the same.

The Penalties of Sin for Adam

Genesis 3:17 And unto Adam he said, Because thou hast hearkened unto the voice of thy wife, and hast eaten of the tree, of which I commanded thee, saying, Thou shalt not eat of it: cursed is the ground for thy sake; in sorrow shalt thou eat of it all the days of thy life;
Genesis 3:18 Thorns also and thistles shall it bring forth to thee; and thou shalt eat the herb of the field;
Genesis 3:19 In the sweat of thy face shalt thou eat bread, till thou return unto the ground; for out of it wast thou taken: for dust thou art, and unto dust shalt thou return.

There are two things to note, when looking at the penalties applied to Adam.

1. The ground is cursed because of you
2. You will return to the ground

1. The ground is cursed because of you

Literal Meaning:
Here we finally get to Adam and his consequences. Now we will severely lack what we really need, food. Originally, he was placed in the garden to tend it, which in this narrative was not hard work. Now, we get thorns and thistles instead of what we want.

However, work has become full of toil and misery and then we die. Wow, that is depressing. Job put it like this, "A man that is born of a woman is of few days, and full of trouble."[20]

What Adam reaped not only affected him, but it disturbed the food sources of all creation. This makes sense, when you recognize the Lord commissioned him, to be the god of this world. Consequently, what affects him will affect everything under him.

Does this make sense? The literal interpretation works here. Adam ate the forbidden fruit and now the source of all of his food is cursed.

Symbolic Meaning:
Symbolically, because Adam (male and female) listened to the people of the Holy City, the repercussions of their actions cursed the ground. Now in sorrow they shall eat of it all the days of their lives. The Hebrew word for ground is "adamah" which is very close to the word for humans (ādām). The wordplay in the Garden of Eden narrative reveals the complex relationship between humans and the earth or ground.

There are so many mentions of the ground that we know it must be an allusion to something else. The ground is a reference for the heart (Jeremiah 4:3, Hosea 10:12). I believe the parable of the Sower is best illustration of Adam's punishment in action.

Matthew 13:18 Hear ye therefore the parable of the sower.
Matthew 13:19 **When any one heareth the word** *of the* **kingdom, and understandeth it not,** *then cometh the wicked one, and* **catcheth away that which was sown in his heart.** *This is he which received seed by the way side.*
Matthew 13:20 But he that received the seed into stony places, the same is **he that heareth the word, and anon with joy receiveth it;**
Matthew 13:21 **Yet hath he not root in himself,** *but dureth for a while: for when tribulation or persecution ariseth because of the word, by and by he is offended.*
Matthew 13:22 **He also that received seed among the thorns** *is he that heareth the word; and* **the care of this world, and the deceitfulness of riches, choke the word,** *and he becometh unfruitful.*
Matthew 13:23 But **he that received seed into the good ground is he that heareth the word, and understandeth it;** *which also beareth fruit, and bringeth forth, some an hundredfold, some sixty, some thirty.*

Because humans hearkened (listened) to the voice of the Woman, over God, the ground of their hearts became hardened (cursed). Now we find it difficult to produce what we need. Jesus plainly tells us the thorns (curse) are the cares of life and deceitfulness of riches.

Christ the last Adam declares by faith we can have not only our needs met, but also our desires.

*Mark 11:23 For verily I say unto you, **That whosoever shall say unto this mountain, Be thou removed, and be thou cast into the sea; and shall not doubt in his heart,** but shall believe that those things which he saith shall come to pass; **he shall have whatsoever he saith**.*
*Mark 11:24 Therefore I say unto you, **What things soever ye desire, when ye pray, believe that ye receive them, and ye shall have them.***

How many people can say they can make these verses work for them, even half of the time? Why is this, the case? It is because of the curse. We must breakup the fallow ground of our hearts, in order to get it to produce what we need and want.

Does this make sense? The symbolic interpretation works as well. Adam (male and female) listened to the Woman over the voice of God and now their ability to access the blessings of the Lord has been greatly afflicted (cursed).

*Jeremiah 17:5 Thus saith the LORD; **Cursed be the man that trusteth in man**, and maketh flesh his arm, **and whose heart departeth from the LORD**.*

Spiritual Meaning:
The symbolic and spiritual meanings are the same.

Does this make sense? Cursed is the ground (heart of humans) because of eating from the tree of good and evil. I believe the apostle Paul shows us the truth of the matter.

Romans 7:15 And I have no clear knowledge of what I am doing, for that which I have a mind to do, I do not, but what I have hate for, that I do.
*Romans 7:16 But, if I do that which I have no mind to do, **I am in agreement with the law that the law is good**.*

64

Romans 7:17 So it is no longer I who do it, but the sin living in me.
Romans 7:18 For I am conscious that in me, that is, in my flesh, there is nothing good: I have the mind but not the power to do what is right.
*Romans 7:19 **For the good which I have a mind to do, I do not: but the evil which I have no mind to do, that I do.***
Romans 7:20 But if I do what I have no mind to do, it is no longer I who do it, but the sin living in me.
*Romans 7:21 So I see a law that, though **I have a mind to do good, evil is present in me.***

I used the Bible in Basic English version, as opposed to the King James, for better clarity. Here we can clearly see the direct effect of eating from the tree of knowledge of good and evil.

Thankfully, Christ has redeemed us from the curse and we are now free.

*Galatians 3:13 **Christ hath redeemed us** from the curse of the law, **being made a curse for us**: for it is written, Cursed is every one that hangeth on a tree:*

The cross is not the only symbolic representation of Christ taking the curse for us. Jesus the last Adam gives us a pictorial illustration and the true location of the ground. Just before He was crucified the Romans placed a crown of thorns on His head, indicating Christ took the curse of Adam upon himself. The imagery is subtle, but unmistakable.

2. You will return to the ground

Literal Meaning:
God declared, instead of work being a joyful source of

purpose and meaning in Adam's life, it would be a lifelong source of necessary frustration. It would be hard and laborious. Moreover, it would end in Adam's eventual death.

God, who formed Adam out of the dust of the ground, announces that Adam will one day die and return to dust. Death would be the final consequence of Adam's choice to sin, just as God had warned when giving the command. Now all humans must live with this curse of death.

Does this make sense? If Adam was the very first human on the planet, this would make sense. It would not clarify why every other living organism dies, but it would explain humanity.

The Bible teaches us that sin came by Adam and death is a product of sin. However, animals do not sin. In addition, everlasting life is never mentioned concerning animals.

Symbolic Meaning:
The implication is humans were not meant to die and death came about through the fall. However, hundreds of thousands of men and women died before God placed Adam in Eden. Therefore, physical death cannot be the issue.

The pictorial illustration is humanity going down to the grave, instead of up with God. The Hebrew wordplay shows us the ground both gives us life and swallows us in death. However, we die in a spiritual sense. The soul never ceases to exist. We have either everlasting life or eternal damnation. Spiritual death or damnation is avoidable. The purpose of the last Adam (Christ) is to restore us, to life eternal.

God is the source of all life. Therefore, separation from Him means death and this is what the writer is implying. Once God fused His Spirit with our frame (dust), the result was an immortal soul. At the point of physical death, the soul of humans is supposed to return to God. This is life eternal. However, because of sin, we have Adam returning to the dust.

Does this make sense? Physical death is part of the cycle of life, but spiritual death is not. God cannot dwell with sin or evil because He is completely holy. Think about it like this, God is light and sin is darkness. Light and darkness cannot coexist. Moreover, God is life and separation from Him is death.

Spiritual Meaning:
The symbolic and spiritual meanings are the same.

The End of Paradise

Genesis 3:20 And Adam called his wife's name Eve; because she was the mother of all living.
Genesis 3:21 Unto Adam also and to his wife did the LORD God make coats of skins, and clothed them.
Genesis 3:22 And the LORD God said, Behold, the man is become as one of us, to know good and evil: and now, lest he put forth his hand, and take also of the tree of life, and eat, and live for ever:
Genesis 3:23 Therefore the LORD God sent him forth from the garden of Eden, to till the ground from whence he was taken.
Genesis 3:24 So he drove out the man; and he placed at the east of the garden of Eden Cherubims, and a flaming sword which turned every way, to keep the way of the tree of life.

Adam named his wife Eve, because she was the mother of all living. Why would he say this, if they were the first people on the planet? Eve is not Adam's mother and she does not have any children at this point of the narrative. Therefore, it is impossible for her to be the mother of all living, if we interpret the story literally. There are so many allusions that tell us Adam and Eve are not the first couple on earth, it is hard to ignore.

In reality, we have Adam both male and female naming the city. They called the name of the place, Eve. This should be the first human civilization. Now, the title "mother of all living", makes perfect sense. The relationship between Eve and Eden is akin to Jerusalem and Israel.

Indicators Adam and Eve were not alone

1. Adam named the animals – meaning language was created already
2. Adam (male and female) is commanded to be fruitful and multiply
3. Eve is called the mother of all living
4. Cain fears people will find and kill him, so God put a mark upon him (Gen 4:14-15)

Next, we see the Lord making skins for Adam and his wife, which means the whole city. We can take two approaches to understanding this passage. First, God made animal skins for the people to wear. Alternatively, He clothed them with human flesh. The first option would entail a great deal of animal killing. This seems to go against the lesson of the tree of knowledge. Therefore, we have God making Adam and his wife mortals. This would be in keeping with the symbolic style of writing.

Adam and the city of Eve are the gods of the earth, by design. They were intended to draw the other hominids to God, just as Israel was supposed to do with the Gentile nations. The city of Eve was the Lord's chosen people. As a result, when they fell in the garden, they became mortals. This of course is only a literary allusion, pointing to their spiritual status.

The shortening of Adam and his descendants lifespan, further highlights their loss of status. Gradually through the generations, the sons of God began to live shorter lives, until we get to the God ordained limit of 120 years.[21] Metaphorically speaking, this is because God prevented access to the tree of life and living forever.

The people and city of Eve descended to mortality and they lost access to the garden. The term mortal does not really capture the essence of what happened. They became carnal, I think better describes it.

Cherubim protect the tree of Life with a flaming sword. Remember, I stated the tree is symbolic of the Word of God. Note, the next time we see Cherubim in the Bible they are guarding the Ark of the Covenant, which contains the Law (Word of God). This is yet another allusion that Israel may be the Garden of Eden.

Now they must till the ground outside of the garden. This forcing out probably was due to food shortages or some climatic condition. Either of these would be a direct consequence of the fall. Now humans have to work hard to get what they need to survive.

Where did God's people go after the Garden of Eden? The cherubim and the flaming sword were placed on the eastside of the garden. Therefore, they migrated east to an undisclosed location, but they were still in the region called Eden. How do we know this? When Cain was cursed and sent away, he dwelt in the land of Nod, east of Eden. Every time humans sin in this narrative, they move eastward, away from God.

This is the story of God's original people and their holy city. The writer wrapped it in an allegory and it has been hidden in plain sight, for centuries. However, this is more than a creation story. It is a prequel of sorts, to the story of Israel.

We have always assumed that Israel was God's original chosen people. Now we can see there were a people God chose before the Israelites. In fact, the call of Abram picks up where the garden story leaves off. Notice, Abram is called by God to relocate just like Adam.

Noted author Dr. Myles Munroe states, "Jesus came to earth to restore what Adam lost, and He brought a kingdom message. Jesus came to reestablish the government of God on earth and to reinstate His earthly kings to their rightful place of dominion. Adam lost a kingdom, not a religion, and therefore the redemptive work of the Creator would be the reestablishment of His Kingdom on earth."[22]

We need to revisit the great mystery that the apostle Paul mentioned in the book of Ephesians. Earlier, I asked the question, is the mystery about a husband and wife in general or does it refer specifically to Adam and Eve?

The Great Mystery

Ephesians 5:22 Wives, submit yourselves unto your own husbands, as unto the Lord.

Ephesians 5:23 For the husband is the head of the wife, even as Christ is the head of the church: and he is the saviour of the body.

Ephesians 5:24 Therefore as the church is subject unto Christ, so let the wives be to their own husbands in every thing.

Ephesians 5:25 Husbands, love your wives, even as Christ also loved the church, and gave himself for it;

Ephesians 5:26 That he might sanctify and cleanse it with the washing of water by the word,

Ephesians 5:27 That he might present it to himself a glorious church, not having spot, or wrinkle, or any such thing; but that it should be holy and without blemish.

Ephesians 5:28 So ought men to love their wives as their own bodies. He that loveth his wife loveth himself.

Ephesians 5:29 For no man ever yet hated his own flesh; but nourisheth and cherisheth it, even as the Lord the church:

Ephesians 5:30 For we are members of his body, of his flesh, and of his bones.

Ephesians 5:31 **For this cause shall a man leave his father and mother, and shall be joined unto his wife, and they two shall be one flesh.**

Ephesians 5:32 **This is a great mystery: but I speak concerning Christ and the church.**

Ephesians 5:33 Nevertheless let every one of you in particular so love his wife even as himself; and the wife see that she reverence her husband.

The Apostle Paul describes marriage as a great mystery in Ephesians 5:32, explaining that marriage is a picture of Christ and the Church, there is no mention of Adam and Eve.

"The term mystery is a common word in the New Testament. Paul uses it 17 times in his letters. Only rarely does it refer to something enduringly mysterious that remains puzzling or uncertain. Rather, mystery typically means what was hidden, concealed, or unclear in the past, but now has been revealed in light of Christ's coming and his gospel. In the gospels, a mystery is not a secret to be kept, but rather a truth that needs to be told."[23]

What is the mystery that Paul talks about and what makes this one so profound? If we look at all of the times the apostle uses the term, we find our answer.

*1 Timothy 3:16 And **without controversy great is the mystery of godliness [the gospel]**: God was manifest in the flesh, justified in the Spirit, seen of angels, preached unto the Gentiles, believed on in the world, received up into glory.*

1. Jesus the son of God came in the flesh
2. He was justified (sinless) in the Spirit
3. He was seen of Angels (heavenly witnesses)
4. Jesus was preached to the Gentiles
5. Believed on in the world (Faith)
6. Returned to God the Father

These six things summarize the mission of Jesus and mystery of the gospel. The long awaited Messiah was not merely a prophet of God, but He was God. Jesus came to earth as a spotless lamb (sinless) to take away the sins of the world. Angels announced His coming into the world and His exit. This is a heavenly witness of the deity of

Christ. The earthly witnesses (disciples) preached Jesus to the Gentiles, after His resurrection. Both Israel and the Gentiles (the world) believed the message of the Gospel. Now the Gentiles are included in the blessings of God with Israel. Through the Messiah, God is no longer the Lord of the Jews only, but of the whole world (Gentiles). Finally, Jesus returned to heaven with God the Father, while His Kingdom is steadily being built here on earth.

How does all of this fit in with the profound mystery of Christ and the Church? Here is the problem. Marriage is not the intended symbol of the mystery. It is the simply part of the narrative. How do we know this is true?

The husband and wife are likened to the human body and the body correlates to Christ and the Church. If we are using the symbolism properly, then all things must be true.

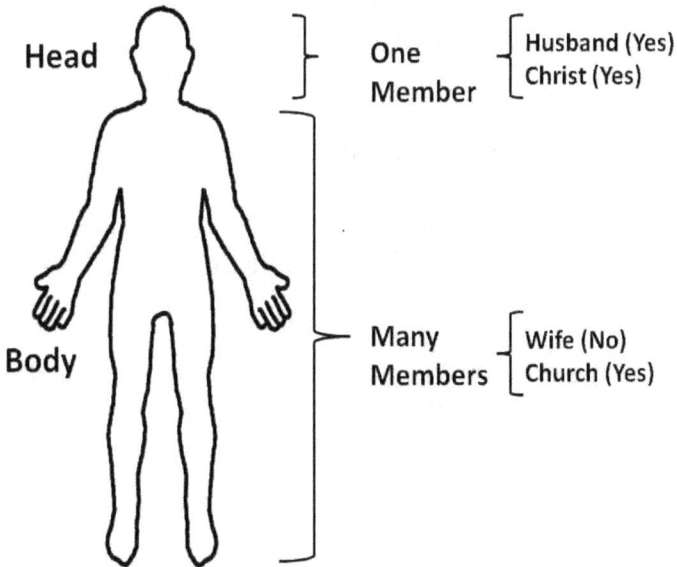

Figure 7. Wife/Body Diagram

As you can see from figure 7, it is true that the husband is equal to one. However, it is not true that the wife is equal to many. It is imperative that all of the symbols match up correctly. The wife cannot equate to many members. Therefore, we have used the symbolism improperly. Let's look at the scripture closer.

Ephesians 5:30 **For we are members of his body, of his flesh, and of his bones.**
Ephesians 5:31 For this cause shall a man leave his father and mother, and shall be joined unto his wife, and they two shall be one flesh.
Ephesians 5:32 **This is a great mystery: but I speak concerning Christ and the church.**

Genesis 2:23 And **Adam said, This is now bone of my bones, and flesh of my flesh: she shall be called Woman,** *because she was taken out of Man.*
Genesis 2:24 Therefore shall a man leave his father and his mother, and shall cleave unto his wife: and they shall be one flesh.

As I stated, marriage (husband and wife) is not the intended symbol of the mystery. Adam and the Woman (Eve) are the true intent. Remember, Adam is both male and female. Again, if we are using the symbolism properly, then all things must be true.

I will use the same illustration and replace the husband with Adam and the wife with the Woman. This way we can see if Adam and Eve are the great mystery.

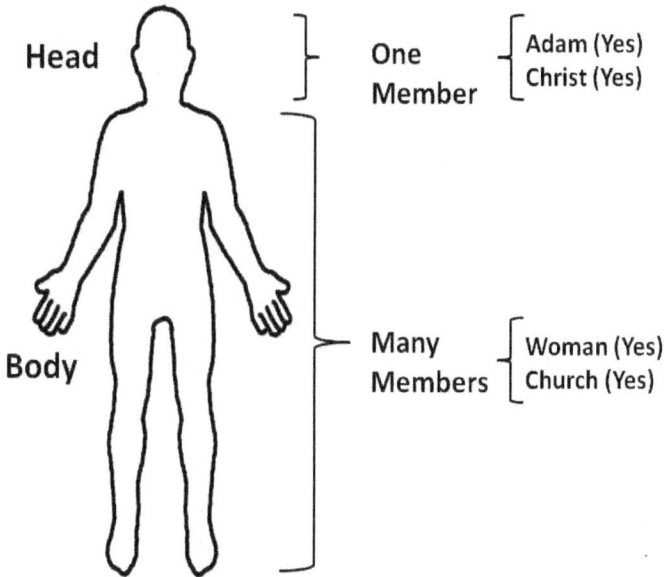

Figure 8. Woman/Body Diagram

As you can see from figure 8, it is true that Adam is equal to one. Wait a minute, if Adam is both male and female, how can they equate to one member? The apostle Paul solved this riddle for us.

*Ephesians 5:31 For this cause shall **a man** leave his father and mother, and **shall be joined unto his wife, and they two shall be one flesh.***

Through the act of marriage, two individuals become one entity (flesh). Therefore, Adam is equal to one member, even though they are technically two separate humans. In addition, it is equally true that the Woman is equal to many. She is the holy city, in other words, the people of God. Now, this arrangement fits perfectly.

Paul's analogy of the Church being the body of Christ proves our assertion, that the Woman is a city and not a literal female. In addition, it serves as another indicator that Adam and Eve were not alone in the Garden.

How did I see this truth, but the apostle Paul did not? Am I greater than Paul? No, that is not the issue. Paul by his own words was a proper Israelite from the tribe of Benjamin. In knowledge of and training in scriptures, he was a Pharisee. He was a Hebrew of the Hebrews (Philippians 3:4-7). His credentials are impeccable. So, what is the issue?

The apostle and I are separated by almost 2000 years, so time is the issue. Paul was not privy to the Bible as we have it today. He only had the Old Testament. He wrote most of the New Testament, but I doubt he kept a copy of it. Furthermore, the book of Revelation was not written until after his death. In it, the Woman gives birth to the man-child, which is Christ (Revelation 12). Additionally, we see the bride is New Jerusalem, which is a slight, but important nuance to the Church (Revelation 21).

Add to all of this, the ability to research everything you want on a computer. I am positive the apostle would have put all of the pieces together, long before I did, if he were alive today.

1 Corinthians 13:12 **For now we see through a glass, darkly;** *but then face to face:* **now I know in part;** *but then shall I know even as also I am known.*

Paul put a huge amount of things together for someone with only partial information and without today's technology. We however, have no excuse. It is imperative that we study to show ourselves approved to God (2 Timothy 2:15).

This is the advice he gave to the younger generation of ministers, like Timothy. So, why are we just now seeing this truth? This is the real question. This is our failing, not Paul's.

What made the mystery profound was the fact that the Gentiles are now included in the body of Christ. This was not common knowledge, as it is now. At the time of Paul's writings, this was a notably new revelation.

Ephesians 3:3 ***How that by revelation he made known unto me the mystery****; (as I wrote afore in few words,*
Ephesians 3:4 Whereby, when ye read, ye may understand my knowledge in the mystery of Christ)
Ephesians 3: ***Which in other ages was not made known unto the sons of men****, as it is now revealed unto his holy apostles and prophets by the Spirit;*
Ephesians 3:6 ***That the Gentiles should be fellow-heirs, and of the same body****, and partakers of his promise in Christ by the gospel:*

Now what makes the mystery even more profound is the fact that it relates to Adam and the Woman (Eve), not a husband and wife. This makes perfect sense when we realize Paul told us that Jesus is the last Adam.

Now that we have a more complete understanding of the mystery, what do we do with Ephesians 5:22-33? We must look at it with new eyes. The wife does not have to submit to the husband. They must work together as one. The book of Amos, asks the question, "Can two walk together, except they be agreed? (Amos 3:3)"

Consequently, the husband is not the head of the wife. However, Christ is the head of the Church and is still an example for both the male and female on how to love each other.   Both the husband and the wife must have a sacrificial love for their spouse.

In marriage, the husband and wife are equal. There is no headship in matrimony, only agreement. This is the will of God from the beginning and His will never changes.[24] The Lord is the same yesterday, today and forever.[25]

I can hear people saying, why didn't Jesus correct things? The meaning of the mystery of the gospel could not be revealed, until after Christ finished His ministry, here on earth.

Women in the Church

There is a vigorous and ongoing controversy over women preachers and pastors, in the United States and all over the world. Many teach that pastoring and preaching are reserved for qualified men only. Others believe this is archaic patriarchal thinking and it has no place in our modern world.

There are scriptures that speak against women being in leadership over men. Unfortunately, no amount of modern thinking can go against the authority of the Bible, no matter how archaic it sounds.

Some say that the conflict over women's authority in the Church has hurt women, making them question themselves and God. Therefore, we need to carefully study and understand what the Bible says about this issue.

There are only two sides to this argument and both have nice sounding names, but unfortunately only one can be right. Those who are for women preachers are called egalitarians and those against it are complementarians.

Egalitarianism, also known as biblical equality, is a Christian theological movement that promotes gender equality and equal responsibilities for all people. It is based on the Christian belief that all people are created in the image of God.

Complementarianism is a theological view that men and women have different, but complementary roles and responsibilities in life. It is based on the idea that God created men and women to reflect complementary truths about Jesus.

Two main passages in the Bible speak against women being in leadership over men. Both are in the New Testament and attributed to the apostle Paul. The first is 1 Timothy 2:11-15 and the second is 1 Corinthians 14:34-35. The first text seems to hold more weight than the second does, so I will make it the main argument.

Paul's Main Argument
1 Timothy 2:11 **Let the woman learn in silence** *with all subjection.*
1 Timothy 2:12 **But I suffer not a woman to teach, nor to usurp authority over the man**, *but to be in silence.*
1 Timothy 2:13 **For Adam was first formed, then Eve**.
1 Timothy 2:14 And **Adam was not deceived, but the woman being deceived was in the transgression**.
1 Timothy 2:15 *Notwithstanding she shall be saved in childbearing, if they continue in faith and charity and holiness with sobriety.*

These verses are the primary reason for women not being allowed in leadership over men. The root of the problem always goes back to Adam and Eve. This scripture is the linchpin argument against women leading men, so let's see if Paul's rationale is actually valid.

Reason 1
Women are not allowed to teach, nor can they usurp (supplant or infringe) authority over a man, but must remain silent. Where did the writer get such a notion?

"The long-standing idea that women are not fit to be educated nor are they fit to be educated have deep roots in

80

Jewish history. Beginning with the Hebrew Bible, the primacy of men is a given and women's status is closely related to their childbearing function."[26]

"The Bible is undeniably steeped in patriarchy. The biblical authors, however, did not invent patriarchy; rather, it was the social umbrella under which the various stories, poems, parables, and priestly proscriptions were written."[27]

As we have seen, everything goes right back to the book of Genesis and the Woman, also known as Eve. However, we have already established that the Woman is not an actual female and that Adam represents both male and female. Therefore, the husband ruling over Eve cannot apply to women. The Woman is the holy city of God and represents His people. So, when we see the husband (Adam) ruling over her. It means that humanity is ruling over the Lord's people, instead of God.

Psalms 81:11 **But my people would not hearken to my voice***; and Israel would none of me.*
Psalms 81:12 **So I gave them up unto their own hearts' lust: and they walked in their own counsels***.*

Genesis 3:16 is not a command to subjugate women, but it is a pronouncement of humanity's sin in the garden. Remember, the Woman represents God's people, not an actual woman.

There is no biblical prohibition against women teaching and being in leadership over men, anywhere in the Bible.

If a woman being in leadership over a man was against God's law or his divine will, then Deborah would not have been a judge over the tribes of Israel. "She was the only female judge in the Bible. Deborah was also a prophet and military leader. She summoned Barak to fight Sisera with 10,000 men, but he refused to go unless she went with him."[28] Barak trusted in the woman of God, more than the word of God. Yet he is listed in the hall of faith (Hebrews 11). None of this could have happened if God actually prohibited women from leadership over men.

1st Support

The first support for Paul's argument, that women cannot teach or usurp authority over a man is based on Adam. The order of creation determines God's hierarchy for the sexes, for Adam was first formed and then Eve. We know from Genesis 5:2 that God created both male and female, calling their name Adam. Furthermore, Adam (male and female) were created in God's image and likeness. Both shared dominion over all of God's creation.[29] Therefore, the male and female were created together, at the same time.

If God through the order of creation intended for men to have authority over women, it would be pointless to curse the woman stating, "Your desire shall be for your husband, and he shall rule over you." If this is a curse, it means originally the situation was different and the man did not rule over the woman.

It is true that Eve was formed after Adam, but she is not a literal woman. Remember, that Eve is God's holy city and she represents the people of God.

Prophecy of the Woman:
*Genesis 3:15 And **I will put enmity between thee and the woman**, and **between thy seed and her seed**; it shall bruise thy head, and thou shalt bruise his heel.*

We see in Genesis chapter three that there is enmity (hostility) between the Woman and the Serpent. In addition, there is opposition between the seed of the Woman and the seed of the serpent. The enmity between the Woman and the serpent is described in more detail in Revelation chapter twelve.

Fulfillment of the Prophecy:
*Revelation 12:1 And **there appeared a great wonder in heaven; a woman** clothed with the sun, and the moon under her feet, and upon her head a crown of twelve stars:*
*Revelation 12:2 **And she being with child cried, travailing in birth**, and pained to be delivered.*
Revelation 12:3 And there appeared another wonder in heaven; and behold a great red dragon, having seven heads and ten horns, and seven crowns upon his heads.
*Revelation 12:4 And his tail drew the third part of the stars of heaven, and did cast them to the earth: **and the dragon stood before the woman** which was ready to be delivered, for **to devour her child as soon as it was born**.*
*Revelation 12:5 And **she brought forth a man child**, who was to rule all nations with a rod of iron: and her child was caught up unto God, and to his throne.*
*Revelation 12:6 **And the woman fled into the wilderness**, where she hath a place prepared of God, that they should feed her there a thousand two hundred and threescore days.*

*Revelation 12:17 **And the dragon was wroth with the woman, and went to make war with the remnant of her seed,** which keep the commandments of God, and have the testimony of Jesus Christ.*

In the book of Revelation, the dragon, also called the old serpent, points back to Genesis. In addition, he is called the

Devil and Satan, just so there is no confusion about the identity of this character.

If the Woman (Eve) is a literal female, then how can she still be alive to give birth to the Messiah, in the book of Revelation? Clearly, the Woman is used symbolically and not literally. Otherwise, this situation would be impossible.

The apostle Paul pointed to the Woman being saved through childbearing, in this same argument against them teaching (1 Timothy 2:15). As I stated in the last chapter, the book of Revelation was written after Paul's death. He did not have the benefit of reading Revelation chapter 12. Otherwise, he would have understood the Woman was symbolic and not a literal female.

Clearly, the Woman mentioned in Genesis 3:15 is the same symbolic representation of the Woman in Revelation 12. She is commonly understood as representing the people of God, thus signifying a connection between the two figures. This is especially true in the context of the "seed of the woman" that will bruise the serpent's head. Therefore, according to Paul, the Woman would have been saved through the birth of Jesus and the curse would have been lifted.

Unfortunately, the apostle Paul was not privy to the book of Revelation. Consequently, we have regulated the Woman to a literal female, instead of the city and people of God. Worse of all, we have built a doctrine on our lack of understanding.

Since, Adam is the term for both male and female, the order of creation argument is irrelevant because Eve is not an actual female.

2nd Support

The second support for Paul's argument, that women cannot teach or usurp authority over a man is based on Eve being deceived and not Adam. Therefore, she becomes subservient to him. This seems like a bit of a reach, as far as justification goes. Think about it. Eve was deceived or tricked into eating the forbidden fruit, but Adam was not. This would suggest that Adam knowingly ate the fruit, which means he willfully sinned. Which is the greater sin?

Hebrews 10:26 **For if we sin wilfully** *after that we have received the knowledge of the truth,* **there remaineth no more sacrifice for sins,**
Hebrews 10:27 **But a certain fearful looking for of judgment and fiery indignation,** *which shall devour the adversaries.*

Even if this line of reasoning made sense, it would not apply to females. Again, ādām is the Hebrew name of both sexes. God is not giving His creation a proper name, but rather He is classifying the species. Today, if we would just say humans that would eliminate a lot of confusion.

Remember, Benson's Commentary, in which he states, "Whereas thou wast made thy husband's equal, thou shalt henceforward be his inferior, and he shall rule over thee — As thy lord and governor."[30] The rationale is they were created equal, but because the Woman ate the forbidden fruit and gave it to her husband, she is now inferior to him and justifiably so. Although this mindset is ingrained in our society, it has absolutely no biblical support.

Additionally, the fact remains that the Woman would have been saved through childbearing, specifically the birth of Christ. Therefore, the curse was removed at the cross.

Galatians 3:13 ***Christ hath redeemed us from the curse*** *of the law,* ***being made a curse for us****: for it is written, Cursed is every one that hangeth on a tree:*

The work of Jesus removed all curses from humanity, not just from the Law. As the last Adam, he brings life and salvation to humanity through his sacrifice, essentially reversing the effects of the first Adam's sin.

The argument that women are not allowed to teach, nor can they usurp (supplant or infringe) authority over a man, but must remain silent in the Church has no scriptural support.

The order of creation is invalid, because Adam represents both male and female (Genesis 5:2). Additionally, Eve being deceived, but not Adam fails for the exact same reason. Consequently, there is no biblical basis for men having authority over women. In the beginning, God made both male and female in His image and in His likeness. The Lord gave them both dominion over the earth, placed them in the garden and together they named the animals and the Woman.

Now that we have thoroughly looked at the main argument used against women being leaders in the Church, let's look at the secondary one.

Paul's Secondary Argument
1 Corinthians 14:34 ***Let your women keep silence in the churches: for it is not permitted unto them to speak; but they are commanded to be under obedience, as also saith the law.***
1 Corinthians 14:35 And if they will learn any thing, let them ask their husbands at home: ***for it is a shame for women to speak in the church****.*

The Law commands silence and women are to be in obedience. It is a shame for women to speak in the Church. If we look at only 1 Corinthians 14:34-35, then we might lose the point of the apostle's message. In isolation, the scriptures seem to indicate that women cannot speak in Church. However, this cannot be the case.

1 Corinthians 11:5 ***But every woman that prayeth or prophesieth*** *with her head uncovered dishonoureth her head: for that is even all one as if she were shaven.*

In chapter eleven of the same letter to the Corinthians, Paul gives us the proper method for men and women to pray and prophesy in Church. Therefore, it is not rationale to believe he is forbidding women to open there mouths in Church in chapter fourteen. After all these scriptures are from the same letter, written to the same church in Corinth.

Galatians 3:27 ***For as many of you as have been baptized into Christ have put on Christ.***
Galatians 3:28 There is neither Jew nor Greek, there is neither bond nor free, ***there is neither male nor female: for ye are all one in Christ Jesus.***

In the spiritual sense, Paul knows there is no difference between male and female. So, what is Paul trying to tell us about women and speaking in Church. He is addressing the social customs of his period. In ancient times, they believed that women were unfit to be educated.

The key to understanding exactly what the apostle Paul is getting at is to read both 1 Timothy 2 and 1 Corinthians 14. Then we can see why he has advocated silence in the churches.

*1 Timothy 2:11 Let the woman **learn** in silence with all subjection.*

*1 Corinthians 14:35 And if they will **learn** any thing, let them ask their husbands at home: for it is a shame for women to speak in the church.*

"When Paul tells women to keep silent, he is not prohibiting their making a verbal contribution to the meeting, whether in the form of praying or prophesying or the like. Rather, he is saying that if they desire to learn anything they should ask their own husbands at home (1 Corinthians 14:35). To do otherwise is improper or shameful."[31]

Why is it shameful for women to inquire and learn in Church? "The role of women in Judaism is determined by the Hebrew Bible, the Oral Law (the corpus of rabbinic literature), by custom, and by cultural factors. Although the Hebrew Bible and rabbinic literature mention various female role models, religious law treats women differently in various circumstances. It was lawful for men in public assemblies to ask questions, or even interrupt the speaker when there was any matter in his speech, which they did not understand; but this liberty was not granted to women."[32]

In addition, there was a strong prejudice in ancient times against women speaking to other women's husbands. Such behavior was strictly taboo. Today these taboos have been removed, for the most part and there is no reason for women to remain silent or not ask questions in Church.

The apostle Paul claims the Law agrees with women remaining silent in Church. However, there is no such law. In Jewish writing neither, the Talmud nor the Torah forbids women from speaking in a synagogue. Paul is using Genesis 3:16 as a precedent for the prohibition.

Genesis 3:16 **Unto the woman he said**, *I will greatly multiply thy sorrow and thy conception; in sorrow thou shalt bring forth children; and thy desire shall be to **thy husband, and he shall rule over thee.***

We have already established that the Woman (Eve) is not an actual female and that Adam represents both male and female. Therefore, the husband ruling over Eve does not apply to women.

The argument that women must remain silent in the Church has no biblical support. There is no such law in the Bible. In addition, the story of Adam and Eve is a symbolic narrative that cannot be taken literally, but it must be properly interpreted.

I know we talked about the apostle Paul having a partial revelation in the previous chapter, but I have another thought on the matter.

I do not think that Paul missed anything. I believe the Lord did not give him the whole revelation. Why would God give Paul only a partial understanding of the mystery of Adam and Eve, in relationship to Christ and the Church?

Here is what I think. I believe God in His wisdom purposely kept part of the mystery hidden. If Paul wrote the whole truth in his letters to the various Churches, then I believe they would have never been included in the canon of the Bible.

Unlike society in ancient Egypt, Rome did not regard women as equal to men before the law. They received only a basic education, if any at all, and were subject to the authority of a man. The Council of Rome canonized the Bible in 382 AD and I highly doubt they would have approved of an egalitarian viewpoint.

"Even during the Renaissance, the life of a woman was subjugation. Her parents controlled a woman throughout her childhood, and then she was handed directly to her husband. A spouse she most likely had not chosen herself, and who would exercise control over her until his or her death."[33] Even during this timeframe, Paul's books could have easily been removed from the Bible. Due to low literacy rates, the majority of people did not have Bibles. It would have hardly been noticed by the masses.

Only during the 19th and 20th centuries did the literacy rates increase enough for the common person to know and understand what was in the Bible. However, women's rights were still a big issue.

Therefore, if Paul had the whole revelation of the great mystery of Christ, his words may have been lost forever and this would have been an immense tragedy for Christianity. However, the time is right today for us to understand the complete truth. In fact, it is overdue.

Before we come to a definitive conclusion, we should look at some of the other arguments against women preaching and pastoring.

Argument 1:
Men and women can have different roles but still be equals. We even see this with the Trinity. The Father, Son and Holy Spirit are equal in essence, yet distinct in their roles when it comes to our salvation.

God did not give separate roles at creation, nor do we see it in the Garden of Eden narrative. Gender roles are a social construct and are culturally determined. They will differ by your locality and change over time. This complementarian theory has its roots in the creation of the Woman (Eve). Genesis 2:18

Argument 2:
After the fall of man, God summoned Adam, not Eve. Romans 5:12-21 says, Adam was held responsible for both of their actions. This is because he was the leader of the two.

Adam is not a proper name in the book of Genesis. The Hebrew term Adam means humans. Eve is the city of God, which is comprised of humans (Adam). Therefore, when the Lord summoned Adam, he called all humans.

Argument 3:
Jesus did not have any female apostles. Instead, they were all male. Jesus was establishing a pattern of male leadership for the entire church age.

This is an illogical argument or logical fallacy. Jesus did not have any non-Jewish apostles either. Does that mean he was establishing a pattern of only Jewish leadership for the entire church age? If so, most of the Church is out of the will of God.

Argument 4:
The biblical qualifications for a pastor imply a person must be a male. Pastor/elders need to be the husband of one wife according to 1 Timothy 3 and Titus 1.

The apostle Paul did not believe women should usurp the authority of a man in Church, based on a literal

91

interpretation of Adam and Eve. So, how would he in the next chapter of the same letter say women could be Bishops and Elders?

However, since the whole premise of men being in authority over women is based on an erroneous interpretation, the entire gender role argument falls apart.

Argument 5:
Women are supposed to be submissive to their husbands because that is God's created order for the family. This comes from Ephesians 5, Colossians 3 and 1 Peter 3. God is concerned about order. In addition, two people cannot be the head of a household.

Wives being submissive to their husbands stems from an improper literal interpretation of Adam and Eve. Ephesians 5 states, "For the husband is the head of the wife, even as Christ is the head of the church: and he is the savior of the body."

This is a logical fallacy called a *False Analogy*. Just because Christ the head of the Church does not mean husbands are the head of the wife. If this were true then, this would mean the husband is the savior of the wife. In addition, the wife would be the body of her husband. Nowhere in the Bible do we find the idea that the husband is the savior of the wife or that she is his body. We looked at this in detail in the last chapter.

As I stated, wives being submissive comes from a flawed literalism of Adam and Eve. However, a solid understanding of the role of husbands and wives should be based on Genesis 1:26, 27. Here the apostle Paul hits the nail on the head.

Galatians 3:28 There is neither Jew nor Greek, there is neither bond nor free, **there is neither male nor female: for ye are all one in Christ Jesus.**

This view harmonizes with the principles of God, perfectly. Every congregation needs to teach and preach this truth.

Argument 6:
There were zero women pastors in the Bible and no women apostles. In addition, there were no women pastors in nearly 2000 years of church history. Therefore, women cannot be pastors.

This argument is the same type as the third one. The *Appeal to Tradition* is a logical fallacy that occurs when someone argues that something is correct because it has been done for a long time, without providing evidence to support it. This argument has no merit.

It is not the intent of this book to answer every argument against women being in leadership. However, I did want to address the ones that prohibited leadership in the Church and see what the Bible really said about the matter.

The misunderstanding of Adam and Eve has caused so much damage and hardship to women. This is why we need to understand the truth of the beginning. We have kept women in bondage for too long. As Jesus stated, "ye shall know the truth, and the truth shall make you free." (St. John 8:32) In the beginning, God made both male and female equal and He has never changed it. To this we should all say, "Amen."

The Bible is clear, but we must take the time to unravel its meaning. Women were not made from men or for them. Adam's help meet is the original Kingdom of God, also known as Eve. In the beginning, God made males and females in His image and gave both of them equal dominion over all of creation and He has never rescinded this decree.

A symbolic narrative should never be interpreted literally, but we have blatantly broken this rule with Adam and Eve. To add insult to injury, we have built doctrines restricting the role of women based on this erroneous interpretation.

The fact that there are still feverish debates about this issue in the 21st century is heartbreaking. It is time to move past our Sunday School understanding of Adam and Eve and finally embrace the truth.

If we continue to oppose women in leadership in the Church, then we are in fact fighting against God, not man. No matter how you feel about the subject, Adam represents both male and female in the book of Genesis. The Bible is clear on this fact.

Robert
Your brother in Christ

<u>Epilogue</u>

I hope that you can see, the way we have understood Adam and Eve, since antiquity has been incorrect. We have subjugated woman purely because of our need to dominate since the Fall and used the Bible as support for it.

Where do we go from here? There are more scriptures that are steeped in a patriarchal tone. It is not my place or my intention to rewrite the Bible. However, I do believe we need to properly understand and apply the scriptures to our lives.

Based on what we now know about Adam and Eve, I think the following scriptures need to be viewed from an egalitarian perspective, instead of the complementarian viewpoint from which they were written.

Colossians 3:18 ***Wives, submit yourselves unto your own husbands***, *as it is fit in the Lord.*
Colossians 3:19 Husbands, love your wives, and be not bitter against them.

There is no longer any biblical support for wives to submit to their husbands. Husbands and wives should both submit themselves to God.

1 Timothy 5:11 ***But the younger widows refuse****: for when they have begun to wax wanton against Christ, they will marry;*
1 Timothy 5:12 Having damnation, because they have cast off their first faith.
1 Timothy 5:13 And ***withal they learn to be idle, wandering about from house to house; and not only idle,***

95

but tattlers also and busybodies, speaking things which they ought not.
*1 Timothy 5:14 I will therefore that **the younger women marry, bear children, guide the house, give none occasion to the adversary to speak reproachfully.***
1 Timothy 5:15 For some are already turned aside after Satan.
1 Timothy 5:16 If any man or woman that believeth have widows, let them relieve them, and let not the church be charged; that it may relieve them that are widows indeed.

I do not know if Churches support widows financially any more. I believe the government has taken on that responsibility. However, some of the language in this text is needlessly patronizing to women. This text should be applied to both men and women.

*Titus 2:3 **The aged women** likewise, that they be in behaviour as becometh holiness, not false accusers, not given to much wine, teachers of good things;*
*Titus 2:4 **That they may teach the young women** to be sober, to love their husbands, to love their children,*
*Titus 2:5 **To be discreet, chaste, keepers at home, good, obedient to their own husbands**, that the word of God be not blasphemed.*

It is a good idea for the older women to teach the younger ones how to navigate marriage and life. However, obedience to their husbands is not a requirement that should be taught. In the same manner, the older men should teach the younger ones how to navigate marriage and life. This is more than proper, it is necessary in today's society.

*1 Peter 3:1 **Likewise, ye wives, be in subjection to your own husbands;** that, if any obey not the word, they also* *may without the word be won by the conversation of the wives;*

1 Peter 3:2 While they behold your chaste conversation coupled with fear.

*1 Peter 3:3 **Whose adorning let it not be that outward adorning of plaiting the hair, and of wearing of gold, or of putting on of apparel;***

1 Peter 3:4 But let it be the hidden man of the heart, in that which is not corruptible, even the ornament of a meek and quiet spirit, which is in the sight of God of great price.

*1 Peter 3:5 **For after this manner in the old time the holy women also, who trusted in God, adorned themselves, being in subjection unto their own husbands:***

*1 Peter 3:6 **Even as Sara obeyed Abraham, calling him lord:** whose daughters ye are, as long as ye do well, and are not afraid with any amazement.*

*1 Peter 3:7 Likewise, ye husbands, dwell with them according to knowledge, giving honour unto **the wife, as unto the weaker vessel,** and as being heirs together of the grace of life; that your prayers be not hindered.*

I have personally seen Churches where it is forbidden to wear makeup, earrings and the like, based on this text. The idea of keeping women plain looking in order to stop men from objectifying them is problematic.

"The root of the problem lies in the culture that often objectifies women, not in how they dress or look. Addressing the issue requires societal change, not individual adjustments by women. Women should have the freedom to express themselves through their appearance without fearing judgment or unwanted attention."[34]

1 Corinthians 11:1 Be ye followers of me, even as I also am of Christ.

97

1 Corinthians 11:2 Now I praise you, brethren, that ye remember me in all things, and keep the ordinances, as I delivered them to you.

1 Corinthians 11:3 **But I would have you know***, that the head of every man is Christ; and* **the head of the woman is the man;** *and the head of Christ is God.*

1 Corinthians 11:4 Every man praying or prophesying, having his head covered, dishonoureth his head.

1 Corinthians 11:5 But every woman that prayeth or prophesieth with her head uncovered dishonoureth her head: for that is even all one as if she were shaven.

1 Corinthians 11:6 **For if the woman be not covered, let her also be shorn: but if it be a shame for a woman to be shorn or shaven, let her be covered.**

1 Corinthians 11:7 For a man indeed ought not to cover his head, forasmuch as he is the image and glory of God: **but the woman is the glory of the man.**

1 Corinthians 11:8 **For the man is not of the woman; but the woman of the man.**

1 Corinthians 11:9 **Neither was the man created for the woman; but the woman for the man.**

1 Corinthians 11:10 For this cause ought the woman to have power on her head because of the angels.

1 Corinthians 11:11 Nevertheless neither is the man without the woman, neither the woman without the man, in the Lord.

1 Corinthians 11:12 For as the woman is of the man, even so is the man also by the woman; but all things of God.

1 Corinthians 11:13 Judge in yourselves: is it comely that a woman pray unto God uncovered?

1 Corinthians 11:14 Doth not even nature itself teach you, that, if a man have long hair, it is a shame unto him?

1 Corinthians 11:15 But if a woman have long hair, it is a glory to her: for her hair is given her for a covering.

1 Corinthians 11:16 **But if any man seem to be contentious, we have no such custom, neither the churches of God.**

This is a long one. First, the head of every woman is not a man; we have debunked this theory already. Paul takes it even further by saying, "the woman is the glory of man because she was created from him." He goes on to say because of this women should have their heads covered when they pray or prophesy. Conversely, men should not have their heads covered when praying or prophesying.

Paul ends his text by saying, if any man has a problem with his advice; this is not a custom of the churches of God. This is true, so I do not know why he felt the need to write about it in the first place.

"In Judaism, the practice of covering the head is a sign of humility before God and an expression of awe before the Divine Presence. It is an ancient tradition that honors God's presence. However, there are no references to covering the head in the Torah, and Jewish law does not explicitly require it."[35]

I hope that this work finally puts an end to the debate over women in Church leadership. There has been so much needless dispute over this issue. Battle lines have been drawn on both sides. I hope and pray that healing can take place and that the love of God will prevail in our hearts.

I am sure there are more scriptures that need to be read or understood in a different in light, because of what we now know about Adam and Eve. This is not a comprehensive list.

I think a good way to get understanding about the scriptures is through Bible studies in your individual Churches or gatherings. My advice to everyone is to be like the Bereans.

Acts 17:11 **Now the Bereans** *were more noble-minded than the Thessalonians, for they* **received the message with great eagerness and examined the Scriptures every day to see if these teachings were true.**

Berean Standard Bible

About the Author

Robert R. Davis is an ordained minister. For over forty years, he has served in a variety of ministries, Sunday school teacher, youth director, minister and Assistant Pastor. He is passionate about the Word, with a gift for looking beneath the surface and understanding the true meaning behind scriptures.

In addition to this work, Robert Davis has written several other books.

- ➤ The Final Message: Understanding the Book of Revelation.

- ➤ In the Beginning: The Truth Behind Genesis

- ➤ 6 Things Every Christian Should Know: The Fundamentals of Christianity

- ➤ What Lies Within: Understanding the Holy Spirit

- ➤ How to Live the Abundant Life

- ➤ Rethink Church

References

[1] Chadad.org. The Curse of Eve. [Online]
<https://www.chabad.org/theJewishWoman/article_cdo/aid/90765/jewish/The-Curse-of-Eve.htm>

[2] Ibid.

[3] National Geographic. Hunter-Gatherer Culture. [Online]
< https://education.nationalgeographic.org/resource/hunter-gatherer-culture/>

[4] History. How Did Humans Evolve? [Online] Updated October 4, 2023. < https://www.history.com/news/humans-evolution-neanderthals-denisovans>

[5] Ibid.

[6] Rutgers. How the Forbidden Fruit Became an Apple. [Online] February 16,2023. < https://www.rutgers.edu/news/how-forbidden-fruit-became-apple>

[7] History. Human Ancestors Tamed Fire Earlier than Thought. [Online] Updated October 3, 2023.
< https://www.history.com/news/human-ancestors-tamed-fire-earlier-than-thought>

[8] Stanford, Craig B. The Hunting Apes: Meat Eating and the Origins of Human Behavior.
< http://press.princeton.edu/titles/6549.html>

[9] History (n 4) .

[10] Studdert-Kennedy, Michael. Language Development from an Evolutionary Perspective.
<http://www.haskins.yale.edu/sr/SR101/SR101_02.pdf>

[11] The Adam and Eve Story: Eve Came From Where? The Biblical Archeology Society. January 2, 2017,
https://www.biblicalarchaeology.org/daily/biblical-topics/bible-interpretation/the-adam-and-eve-story-eve-came-from-where/

[12] Scientific Research. Open Access. [Online]
<https://file.scirp.org/Html/8-1760197_49227.htm>

[13] Social Creatures. The Evolution of Social Connection as a Basic Human Need. [Online] May, 24 2024.
<https://www.thesocialcreatures.org/thecreaturetimes/evolution-of-social-connection>

[14] Davis, Robert. The Final Message. Understanding the Book of Revelation. (Connecticut: Kingdom Works Publishing, 2008) p. 80

[15] Ibid.

[16] Holy Bible. St. Luke 7:34.

[17] Ibid.

[18] Got Questions. How is a woman's desire for her husband a curse (Genesis 3:16)? [Online]
<https://www.gotquestions.org/desire-husband-rule.html>

[19] Bible Hub. Genesis 3:16. [Online]
<https://biblehub.com/commentaries/genesis/3-16.htm>

[20] Holy Bible. Job 14:1.

[21] Holy Bible. Genesis 6:3.

[22] Munroe, Myles. Rediscovering the Kingdom. Ancient Hope for our 21st Century World. (Shippensburg, PA: Destiny Image Publishers, Inc., 2004) p. 64.

[23] Desiring God. What is the Mystery of Marriage? [Online] July 11,2018. <https://www.desiringgod.org/articles/what-is-the-mystery-of-marriage>

[24] Holy Bible. Malachi 3:6.

[25] Holy Bible. Hebrews 13:8.

[26] Jewish Women's Archive. Learned Women in Traditional Jewish Society. [Online] <https://jwa.org/encyclopedia/article/learned-women-in-traditional-jewish-society>

[27] T.J. Wray. The Lives and Roles of Women in Biblical Times. [Online] <https://tjwrayauthor.com/the-lives-and-roles-of-women-in-biblical-times/>

[28] Jewish Women's Archive. Deborah: Bible. < https://jwa.org/encyclopedia/article/deborah-bible>

[29] Holy Bible. Genesis 1:26-28.

[30] Bible Hub. Genesis 3:16. [Online]
<https://biblehub.com/commentaries/genesis/3-16.htm>

[31] Sam Storms. Does Paul Require the complete silence of women in Church? A Study of 1 Corinthians 14:33b-35. < https://www.samstorms.org/enjoying-god-blog/post/does-paul-require-the-complete-silence-of-women-in-church-a-study-of-1-corinthians-1433b-35>

[32] Google Search AI. (2024). The role of women in judaism.

[33] Spark Notes. Italian Renaissance (1330-1550). [Online]
<https://www.sparknotes.com/history/european/renaissance1/section9/>

[34] Google Search AI. (2024). Keep women plain looking to stop men from.

[35] Google Search AI. (2024). Jewish men pray with their heads covered.